The Shut the Fu*k Up Method

Silence your way to the life of your dreams

Jorge Perez

in this book. Always consult with a professional before making any significant changes to your health, lifestyle, or financial practices.

First Edition

Cover design by Happy Ali
Illustration by Abhinav Verma
Editing by Lisa Duncan
Advisor: JR Invina

979-8-21841-459-7

To my parents, Yolanda Angelica Zumaeta and Jorge Osvaldo Perez. I love you with all my heart. Your love and generosity made me who I am today. You better save me a good seat up there... I have the best stories for you.

The Guest House

This being human is a guest house. Every morning a new arrival. A joy, a depression, a meanness, some momentary awareness comes as an unexpected visitor. Welcome and entertain them all! Even if they're a crowd of sorrows, who violently sweep your house empty of its furniture, still treat each guest honorably. He may be clearing you out for some new delight. The dark thought, the shame, the malice, meet them at the door laughing, and invite them in. Be grateful for whatever comes, because each has been sent as a guide from beyond.

Rumi, translated by Coleman Barks

Acknowledgment

Writing this book has been a journey of self-discovery, love and growth, and I am deeply grateful to everyone who has supported me along the way.

First and foremost, I would like to express my gratitude to my sister Vanessa Perez for being my best friend. She is my inspiration of what a perfect human could be. I am so happy you were my partner in crime as we helped our parents transition to heaven.

I am indebted to my family, friends and colleagues who provided invaluable feedback, inspiration, and encouragement. Your insights and support have been instrumental in shaping this book and my life.

I want to extend my heartfelt thanks to Alex Abreu, Happy Ali, Beatriz Alvarez, Tamara Bakir, Lance Bass, Gabby Bernstein, Lauren Bryant, Steve Buck, Erica Cornwall, Gerry Conedy, Mauricio Cruz, Dayana Davila, Maytee Davis, Jamil Damji, Lisa Duncan, Adilia Escamarone, Dora Elizalde, Barry Funkmaster,

Francia Fusik, Tarek El Moussa, Brittny Gastineau, Silvio Horta, Natividad Houxwell, JR Invina, Chad Kolarcik, Yadira Leon, Carolina Levy, Paola London, Diana Madison, Lynn Martinez, Maria F. Martinez, Heather McDonald, Krystal Mendez, Massiel Miranda, Stuart O'Keeffe, Paola Paulin, Carlos Perez, Carlos Perez Sr, Hortensia Perez, Jose Perez, Juan Perez, Juan Perez Sr, Trina Perez, Morgan Portman, Josh Reed, Selina Ringel, Tanya Rollery, Kelly Sprague, Rosana Suarez, Bridget Trama, Patricia Velasquez, Agata Zumaeta, Carlos Zumaeta and Pablo Zumaeta for their expertise and guidance. Your wisdom and support have been invaluable to me.

A very special thank you to my Book Fairy Godmother... Nichola. I am so humbled and grateful for your belief in me.

I am also grateful to my incredible mentors Byron Katie and Dr. Joe Dispenza who have shaped my way of seeing and understanding life. Your openness and vulnerability have inspired me to keep pushing forward and striving to make a difference.

Finally, I want to thank God, the universe and YOU the reader. I am humbled and grateful for the chance to share my journey with you.

With love and gratitude,

Jorge

Foreword

J orge Perez's STFU method is a deeply moving and heartfelt guide for getting out of one's own way. It's hard to imagine how one can recover from the trauma of losing not one but two parents to cancer. Jorge teaches how we can all be our own healer and how we are much more powerful than society and cultural norms have allowed us to believe. Join Jorge as he discovers the secret truth that we are all our own medicine.

-Jamil Damjil

Table of contents

Introduction

S hut the fuck up...is the key to happiness

March 13, 2022, 4:22 am. My mom — my best friend just died in my arms. She fought a hard battle with breast cancer that metastasized to her brain. The hospice nurse is in the room next to me. She just got on the phone to arrange for my mom's body to be picked up. This is so surreal. I can't believe this is my life. My father just died of cancer too, three years ago. His cancer was Leukemia. I was his stem cell donor. My stem cells didn't take. My dad was 67 years old, and my mom was 70 years old. They died young.

Two weeks after my mom's death, I called my sister Vanessa, who is my other best friend and only sibling. I told her that if she ever went to the doctor and got any kind of cancer scare, we would go do a retreat with Dr. Joe Dispenza. Dr. Dispenza is a doctor who focuses on epigenetics, the study of how our environment (both internal and external) affects our health. His meditation retreats have been documented to have helped people heal from cancer.

My priority became the study of epigenetics. I dove deep into the work and learned that genetic predispositions are like firecrackers. You can have firecrackers in your house and if you don't light them, they are not going to explode. What turns on our genetic predisposition? Stress and being in a state of fight-or-flight.

I became obsessed with my parents' death and studied what could have gone wrong. After digging deep, I learned that my father lived with rage about the economic collapse of his business in Venezuela. My mom, on the other hand, lived with so much trauma from her childhood and divorce from my father. Both of them innocently lived in fight-or-flight too much of their lives. Eventually, their poor bodies couldn't take it anymore. Their fragile immune systems collapsed and gave in to cancer.

My passion became to make sure that my sister and I wouldn't have their fate. I got deep into meditation. I got my sister really into it too. The benefits from meditating have changed both my sister and me. It made us calmer, lighter in our minds and physically healthier.

Studies show that people are currently living 70% of their lives in fight-or-flight stress, which is not sustainable for the human body. We need to shift NOW before the epidemic of stress gets even worse. After 25 years of being in the personal development space, I noticed that there was a big common denominator of why people would stay stuck; they couldn't SHUT THE FUCK UP about the complaints in their lives. If you are still complaining about your boss, your kids always leaving a mess, or how your mother-in-law is always judging you...you are staying stuck in your life.

Now, I am not saying not to take action when there is a problem. I encourage you to take action immediately if needed. I also think that grieving a loss of any kind is necessary for the soul. The grieving process is subjective for all of us. And yet, at the same time, the correlation between the quality of our lives and what we constantly talk about, is self-evident.

When we dwell on something for too long, we get stuck in a thought pattern, an emotional roller coaster. Telling everyone about a problem will not help your cause. We don't need to overshare to feel understood. But speaking to one good friend or one professional therapist about your situation could be your greatest solution.

We have to be careful of the slippery slope of complaining. We need to start to carefully listening to what we say to ourselves and others (even if nobody is listening). Have you noticed how many times you say that something is "hard?" Think about it for a moment. Is something really "hard" or is this an emotional habit/addiction that we picked up somewhere along the way? When we are telling everyone how much we don't like our life...that's when we need to shut the fuck up. The STFU Method provides a road map to reverse-engineer your life; to truly transform it from the inside out.

This book is about transforming how we metabolize stress. I make it really simple. The only way we will transform our lives is to stop complaining, period. But don't worry, I will give you the tools for how we can all stop our complaining addiction right away.

I had a huge epiphany about how I personally metabolize stress when leaving a yoga retreat a few years ago. I was at the airport in Guatemala walking to my flight. I had never felt so holy, magical, and mystical. I was returning to Los Angeles after being in a mind-blowing, one-week meditation and yoga retreat. I was feeling so connected to Mother Earth and my purpose in life. When I made it to the ticket counter, I was smiling from ear to ear. All of a sudden, Gloria, the Guatemalan ticket agent, informed me that my reservation had been canceled, and they couldn't reschedule my flight for two days.

In that moment, all my meditation and holy love went out the window. Rage, panic, and fear took over my body. My complaining escalated into verbal aggression. It went from "You have made a huge mistake" to "I need to speak with your manager" to "You are useless." How was it that I couldn't use what I learned in my meditation retreat? I couldn't find a way to control my anger and just shut the fuck up.

This insight, that I was so wired to complain, was the genesis of this book. I had to learn to rewire my frustrations. I am not saying that we need to ignore difficulties when they happen. My intention is for you to be mindful of what you say in everyday life. If you do this, little by little you will transform everything. Not only will you feel more at peace when "bad things" happen, but you will attract more of what you want.

The power of disruption is available to all of us. You just have to do your part. Congratulations! You have found the key to transforming your life. And it all starts with the STFU Method.

ONE

Heal Faster, Help Faster

❞ *The Universe is always conspiring to support you, guide you, and lead you compassionately toward the highest good."*

- Gabby Bernstein

What does healing look like? Healing looks different for each of us. In my experience, when I can think back on a once painful event without feeling hurtful emotions, that's healing.

Life is going to happen to all of us. And yes, some of us are going to lose loved ones to cancer. Some of us are going to lose the love of our lives. And some of us will lose our health or even a child. When I say "lose," I mean it as the completion of a cycle, whether that's by someone or something going away or dying.

But what if that "horrible" loss that we are so scared of can also be our greatest catalyst for healing? The kind of healing that will affect and heal people all around us.

The other day I was talking to one of my best friends, Mark. We both lost our parents to cancer. Having lost both our parents made us able to offer help to other people through our stories, allowing us to become examples of vulnerability and strength.

I am not saying that everyone who has been through a loss should think about becoming a motivational speaker. Yet, I do find it interesting that so many people who have suffered loss and grief have turned their path into service. At the core, we are all wired to help, to be of service to humankind.

When we overcome a massive loss, whether it's physical or emotional, we serve as the "four-minute mile." When the first person in history broke the first four-minute mile running, everyone else started doing it after. But it took one person to do it first. It took one person to show us it was possible.

When I refer to overcoming something like a loss, a physical challenge, or an emotional challenge, it doesn't need to look like anything specific. Meaning, that once we get to a place where we feel at peace with our current situation, we are healed.

I was at a retreat once where I met a man who had ALS (Amyotrophic Lateral Sclerosis), a neurological disease that inhibits your body's motor skills. He was at peace with his ALS condition, and he told me that he was way happier than in his former days when he had full body motion control, but was depressed. For him, living successfully with ALS was being in a state of wholeness, regardless of his ALS diagnosis or symptoms. To him, this was true freedom.

Everyone's process is perfect. We all have our way of dealing with a difficult time. For myself, overcoming the loss of my parents was important on many levels. It served as my example of how the human spirit prevails and was the catalyst for me to pursue a path of healing and to put this information out there into the world. I am here to be of service with my life experiences, and I know that I am not the only one. If you are one of my kind, I see you. And thank you for joining me on this STFU Method journey.

TWO

The STFU Method and 10 Commandments

> **❝** *There is no way to happiness, happiness is the way."*
>
> *- Wayne Dyer*

The STFU Method is a transformative approach that emphasizes the power of silence and self-reflection to radically improve one's life. It revolves around the understanding that excessive complaining, dwelling on problems, or engaging in negative self-talk perpetuates stress and impedes personal growth. By adopting the STFU Method, we reverse engineer: "Believe, thought, word," and we go backwards. We stop the words, which will minimize the thoughts, thus eradicating the beliefs. Individuals will learn to quiet their minds, focus on positive affirmations, and engage in practices that promote a healthier, more optimistic outlook on life. This method is not about suppressing one's voice but about harnessing the power of strategic silence to detox from negativity, rewire one's thought patterns, and ultimately lead a more fulfilled and peaceful life.

The STFU Method 10 commandments- The core of the method

1. Thou shalt not use a person's name when talking shit about them.

When discussing others unfavorably, refrain from using their names. Instead, refer to them as "my friend" to maintain anonymity.

2. Thou shalt only talk about your problems to one chosen person(s).

Limit verbal expression of personal troubling issues to one trusted confidant. Precede each discussion by explicitly stating that they will be the only person that will hear this story. This will create a powerful bond between the both of you.

3. Thou shalt not partake in gossip except just to add "I hear you."

In situations where gossip arises, remain silent or simply acknowledge it with "I hear you." Avoid contributing to negative discussions about absent individuals. When speaking about individuals not present, ask yourself: "What would they think if they could hear you right now?"

4. Thou shalt practice generosity when listening.

Allow others the freedom to express themselves, even if their words are negative.

5. Thou shalt be compassionate in their own narrative of a problem.

Maintain a compassionate outlook when speaking or thinking of your own challenges.

6. Thou shalt not be a reporter.

Remind yourself that you're not a TV reporter. Frame descriptions of events from a perspective aligned with your desired outcomes rather than how the world perceives them. Be intentional about what you say and what you want to see in the world.

7. Thou shalt listen and not just wait for your turn to talk.

Listen intently without merely waiting for your chance to speak. Strive to listen twice as much as you talk and refrain from dominating conversations.

8. Thou shalt remember that millions of people would love to be in your shoes.

Keep in mind the abundance of blessings in your life and maintain a perspective of gratitude. Recognize that many would eagerly trade places with you, fostering appreciation in all aspects of life.

9. Thou shalt remember that life is temporary.

Acknowledge the transient nature of existence consistently. Remain mindful that life is fleeting, and one's time on Earth is finite, urging a sense of urgency and purpose.

10. Thou shalt remember to shut the fuck up before telling anybody else to shut the fuck up.

Before telling anybody what to do, remember that everyone is right about their own decision-making for themselves. Use empathy at all times when interacting with others.

THREE

Detox Your Mind

> **❝** *It's not the problem that causes our suffering; it's our thinking about the problem.* ”
>
> *- Byron Katie*

We're all emotionally addicted to our lives. What I mean by that is that there's a chemical reaction happening to all of us at every moment. We don't pick and choose our experiences; we're energetically attracted to them. Haven't you noticed how you have that one friend that always dates the same kind of guy? Or that you always seem to have the same issue with different people? It's not the issue that is the problem, the problem is that we keep perpetuating the issue by continually talking about it.

Studies show that the subconscious mind runs 95% of what happens to us. That means that our belief system is running automatically and running the show. Inevitably, how we see the world is how we experience it, and how we see people is how we experience them.As a culture, we have normalized complaining and bitching, and we have paid a hefty price for it, the deterioration of the quality of our lives. If you knew that bitching about people and complaining about your boss just keeps them behaving that way, would you still do it?

Let's say you are in your work environment and you and your co-workers have normalized complaining about your boss. You have even created a bonding ritual to complain about him with your co-workers around the water cooler. But isn't it interesting that you keep experiencing your boss the way that you describe him? I am not talking about not addressing an issue that you might have with him and going straight to the source. I am talking about when you go around telling everyone he is a nightmare. Sure, it might get you some brownie points and a few laughs, but the price that you are paying is the quality of your life (since at the end, you are the one experiencing a nightmare boss).

Also, keep in mind that when we have a problem with somebody, it most likely means that we are not being compassionate with that person. I am not saying that you are not right about your boss, but if you knew how he came genetically wired into this world and the issues he has at home, would you still complain about him? If you knew that telling everyone that he is a nightmare is what keeps you experiencing him that way, would you still do it?

I know people think that they are "getting things off their chest" by talking about them, but are they, really? After they tell the tenth person in one day do you really think they are getting something off their chest? Or do you think they are playing out an emotional addiction that they have about complaining? There is nothing wrong with complaining...if you want to keep experiencing the same things that you don't want in your life.

You may not want to hear this, but you might want to take a look at some friendships that you have in your life. Are they based on the two of you bitching? You may think that you are bonding with your friend, but in reality, you are both emotional drug addicts doing the drug of complaining together. Sure, you are going to feel great while you are on your "high" of bitching. But the minute you run out of that feeling; another "bad boss" is going to come out of nowhere and take you on that roller coaster high again. This is all because your body craves that dynamic subconsciously.

Our observations affect reality. This part right here is the core of this book. YOU are the observer and you get to determine what you observe and the way you observe it. The days of being a "news reporter" are over, we can no longer afford to look at the world and simply describe what we see. This way of living could be called "World/Word." You see the world and then you describe it. The upgraded version of this is reversing the order to "Word/World." This means that you describe the world as you want to see it (this is a little gem I picked up from Landmark Education, a personal development program).

I am not saying for you to look at your bank account and scream: "I am rich!" (if that's not true.) But you don't have to call up all your friends and tell them that you are broke either. Where you put your attention energy grows. It is that simple. Some people think that it might be careless to not pay attention to the problem -- as if talking about the problem consistently and commiserating over your issues (and the issues of the world) is a valid way of being. But it doesn't quite work that way.

I'm all about the law of attraction and how our focus shapes our reality. It's like this magnetic force that draws to us whatever we consistently put our energy into. So, when there's a challenge, it's important to address it, no doubt. But dwelling on it endlessly, just rehashing the same problem over and over again, isn't productive. It's like trying to fix a leaky boat by constantly bailing out water without actually patching the hole. Sure, acknowledging the issue is the first step, but then it's time to shift focus towards finding solutions and taking action. That's the real key to making things change for the better.

FOUR

We Are Not Reporters

> ❚❚ *You've just got to ignore the gossip and focus on what's important to you."*
>
> *- Lance Bass*

Ever watch the news? I hope you are saying NO, but we know that you do. I am not saying not to be informed about current events. In case you didn't notice, we could still find out about everything that happens in the world even if we don't watch the news. So, imagine that somewhere along the way in life we have all become reporters. And it doesn't matter if it's for CNN or Fox News, it's all the same. We gather around reporting what we see and describing it.

Describing the world as we see it its part of the "World/Word" phenomenon. We don't see things as they are, we see things as we are. I know you probably think, "But wait, if something looks like shit or looks dangerous, the whole world will agree that there is a problem." But then my question is do you want to be right, or do you want to be happy? Because if you want to be right you could agree with the whole world, but if you want to be free and fully take on leaving "the MATRIX," then keep reading.

If we look inside a cell with a microscope, we are going to find chaos. In a chaotic environment, bacteria thrive and out of that environment, cells are made. Could it be that at our most primal level, there needs to be chaos for harmony to rise? Consider the "Big Bang" theory. Out of the most explosive chaos the most perfect order was created, the universe.

Now let's look at a more everyday example, you are renovating your house. There is going to be a time during the renovation when everything is going to look very chaotic. If you took a screenshot of that reality and called it "Life," then life would seem like a mess. But alas the reality is that the mess you are seeing is part of the order that is being created. It needs to go through the mess first.

If we start looking at all the chaos in the world with this new perspective, that there is a necessary mess involved with any resolution and harmony of any situation, we might feel differently about what is going on. And that's the key right there, if we start feeling differently about what is going on (even if it's just in a subtle way), then we are going to start feeling better. If we start feeling better, then we are going to start attracting another reality of the situation and producing different thoughts altogether.

Everything is energy and if we are seeing a lot of chaos in the world, that means that we have an active pattern about what is happening (and there is nothing wrong with that). As we start softening the story of what we are seeing, we are going to start attracting different things. While this may sound like suggesting that individuals in impoverished regions have somehow brought their circumstances upon themselves, I assure you, that's not my intention. There are complexities beyond our comprehension, such as the interplay between free will and destiny, or the mysteries of life's inherent inequalities. Our best bet is to look at our current situation with a clean slate and say: "This is where I am, and where do I want to go."

Committing ourselves to seeing what is wrong in the world is part of the human survival tendency that we came wired with. And/or is a habit or addiction that we picked up somewhere along the way. To break out of this cycle we have to speak about the world the way that we want to see it.

Consider how, in many instances, we find ourselves upset by situations or individuals simply because we fail to view them from a different perspective. Often, we presume that altering the situation or person would bring us greater contentment. But can we truly be certain? How can we know if navigating through such circumstances won't ultimately guide us to precisely where we need to be.

We often go about convinced that we understand how life ought to unfold, yet the reality is quite different. What if we approached every endeavor with unwavering enthusiasm, acknowledging that we don't always know what's best for us? While there are moments when it seems we lack control, I firmly believe that we retain a degree of influence through our perspective.

We have complete control over our perspective and the way we recount the events that shape our lives. While I acknowledge that our narrative tendencies are influenced by factors such as programming, culture, and the subconscious, my focus lies in refining this narrative framework. I'm fascinated by the prospect of cleansing our programming to empower ourselves with the ability to shape our life's narrative.

The concept behind this book, The STFU Method, serves as our initial stride toward refining the narrative of our lives. As we refrain from default speech patterns, our mental wiring undergoes a transformation. It's like purging ourselves of emotional dependencies that shape our perspectives. Initially, abstaining from participating in complaints or gossip may feel foreign amidst a backdrop of societal norms. Yet, as you persist in avoiding negative discourse, the process becomes progressively easier. It's like embarking on a detox journey, just like a drug addict's first day in rehab. While day one may present the greatest challenge, with each passing day and display of will power, transformative shifts occur. Former sources of irritation begin to lose their potency or simply dissipate. Life assumes a dream-like quality, brimming with positivity. Those who no longer align with your journey naturally fade away, while beauty reveals itself in myriad forms.

Our brains are literally computers. We have been programmed through genetics, culture, environment, and habits. And, who knows...maybe some past life shit too (if you believe in that). The good news is that it doesn't matter how we got programmed. The even better news is that we can re-program ourselves. Now, for me, there are only two ways to re- program (and both ways must be done for it to work). I am going to make this easy for you.

1. Meditation- When you meditate, especially in the morning right when you wake up or at night before you go to sleep, your brain is in the state of theta. When your brain is in theta, you are highly suggestible. If you use a guided meditation that is filled with positive affirmations (I love Dr. Joe Dispenza's meditations) you will literally reprogram your brain with positive ways of being. If you keep this practice going for a while, just like working out your body at the gym, your muscles will start to show. All of a sudden you will start losing your desire to be negative. You will worry less, you will be less suspicious of people, and you'll start being a "half glass full" type of person. For me the most exciting stuff was when someone would cut me off on the road and I noticed that I hardly got mad, maybe out of a

scale of 1- 10, I got to a 3, and then I quickly would shake it off. That's what got me the most excited. But this is not enough. To completely do the rewiring you must do the below part too.

2. SHUT THE FUCK UP- LOL... I am not kidding. You are doing the mental exercise of meditation (consider this is like going to the gym) but if you don't eat properly, drink protein, and rest (shutting the fuck up) your efforts will not be optimized for effectiveness. The STFU method is just as important as meditation. What I mean is that life will put you in situations where people are going to gossip, people will be negative, etc. You must summon your willpower to not participate in these conversations. Listen, I am also not saying that you need to give a mouthful to everyone who is speaking negatively around you and be "the STFU police." But you don't have to add to that conversation. You could just smile and nod, they probably won't even notice that you are not jumping in on the bashing, but YOU will, and that's all that matters. Sometimes when people want agreement on shit talking about someone I even say: "I hear you," like, I literally hear words coming out of your mouth.

When I started the STFU Method at the beginning I had very little patience when people started gossiping, being negative or talked bad about people. I found myself hanging up on people rapidly on the phone or giving them a mouthful about how they were perpetuating their negative situation by talking the way they were. But then as I continued this path, I started to become intimate with the concepts of "compassion" and "acceptance" towards myself and others.

In reality at the beginning of my personal process, I was finding myself trying to control the situation in the name of "positivity" and being "right." Control is one of the biggest default settings that we have as human beings. Once I got to detox more and more through meditation and the STFU method, I lost the need to try to control the way that other people spoke. I started to find it adorable that they were negative and found them too amusing to even try to control or change them at all.

Some of my friendships did change, and some people faded out of my life. I wasn't holding up a torch saying I was better than them or more spiritually evolved. I just became clear that they needed to do their thing over there and I needed to do my thing over here.

No one is doing better than anyone; we are just all on different paths. There are people whom I dearly love with all my heart, and I know that we should keep our distance. The thing is, when you hang out with a person who is constantly talking badly about other people or sharing their secrets, what do you think they are doing behind your back? Exactly. I started to tell those people less and less personal stuff until there was nothing left to say. Now, I know they weren't doing it on purpose, this is all subconsciously wired behavior, but it also doesn't mean that I need to keep them around either. The curious thing is that I felt a lot of love and compassion for those people. When a person is gossiping negatively about someone to create comradery and relatedness in a group, do you know what happens when that person is left alone with no one to gossip about? What do you think? Take a guess. That person starts to attack themselves. I am not a religious person, but in this case the Bible kind of has it right: "Love thy neighbor like you love thyself." If I hate you, I hate me.

As I consistently strive to "speak clean" about others, I find myself naturally adopting a more compassionate and accepting tone towards myself. As we age, the reflections we see in the mirror may not always be flattering, so fostering a habit of positive speech becomes increasingly vital.

F I V E

Declare Your Vision

66 *I believe that every action, every decision we make should be intentional. It's about being present in the moment and understanding the impact of our choices on ourselves and others."*

-Patricia Velasquez

What if I told you that your world is just your belief system played out in the 3-dimensional realm? Pretty wild, right? I know this is where my friends think that I am really annoying, but it's true. Whether consciously or subconsciously, we control the way we experience the world.

To become a deliberate creator, meditation is crucial. Yet, I realize that for some, this term can be perplexing or even triggering. The concept of shutting one's eyes and purposefully remaining awake might seem strange at first. But trust me, after a while, you can connect with the magic of the world. If you are starting out with meditation, I would recommend doing it for five or ten minutes at the most. I also recommend using guided meditations where you can hear a waterfall or nature sounds. Let's face it: sitting in complete silence for more than five minutes is hard if you've never done it before. Also, where do you find a completely silent moment? Plus, your nervous system is not used to being in silence and it might feel too foreign for it.

There are a ton of free guided meditations that you can get on YouTube, and you can even specify how many minutes you want to meditate for. I think the Calm app is great for beginners, and Dr. Joe Dispenza guided meditations are my favorite "go-to" guided meditations.

Let me be frank with you, and I understand if it's not what you want to hear, but establishing a solid meditation practice is imperative if you want to re-wire your subconscious habits. It's the key to regulating your nervous system, and it's a fundamental preparation for embracing the STFU Method. While it's not impossible to grasp the STFU Method without a consistent meditation practice, having one will greatly enhance your journey. I'll delve into the significance of maintaining a balanced nervous system and keeping the "fight-or-flight" response in check, later in this chapter.

The optimal times for meditation are either in the morning or right before bed. During these periods, your brain enters the theta state, its most receptive state for re-wing it. This is crucial because many of us harbor hidden negative core beliefs and meditating at this time is basically like going into the "hardware" of the brain. By "negative," I don't imply moral judgment; rather, these beliefs are rooted in survival instincts.

Consider our past - being human was daunting just a few generations ago. Our ancestors lived in eras of limited medical advancements, and the world was considerably more primitive. It's a tough reality, but that's how it was. I am sorry kiddo.

The "fight-or-flight" survival mechanism is innate to all of us, passed down through generations from ancestors who faced extreme conditions. Ever wondered why little kids fear the dark? It's not learned behavior; it's ingrained in their DNA. Predators often strike in darkness. Our instincts warn us of potential danger. Isn't it remarkable? It's as though our genetic memory recalls our ancestors being prey to Saber-toothed tiger. Now, we're like, "No way, I am not going to end up as a snack this time.

Let's break it down. Meditation is like the ultimate chill pill for calming that fight-or-flight impulse, so we're not constantly on edge. Here's a reality check: Ever noticed how we're drawn to "bad news"? It's because our fight-or-flight instinct whispers that knowing what's wrong in the world keeps us safe. So, don't point fingers at CNN or Fox News for dishing out "bad news" — it's what we crave. We convince ourselves we need to stay informed for safety's sake. But guess what? The more news we consume, the more stressed we get. And guess what else? Stress weakens our immune system, making us more vulnerable to sickness. Here's the ultimate kicker: That alarm system we're born with, fight-or-flight, It's the same one that ironically ends up killing us... MIC DROP!

You know what's interesting? We can't even blame advertisers like Apple or Toyota for capitalizing on CNN's high ratings during the 10 O'clock news—especially when that's the time CNN reports on the war. It's like advertisers see those numbers and think, "Great, let's keep supporting this."

News stations are businesses, after all. They are in the business of being seen by eyeballs, and that's what they intend to keep doing. They are not in the business of keeping track of our personal stress and the potential harm that watching the news could do to us.

Once you've harnessed the power of calming your nerves, you're primed for the STFU Method, and I bet you're wondering, "What in the world does that mean?" Trust me, it's rooted in science. Picture this: You enter a room, glance left, and what do you see? Chaos. The floor's littered, trash everywhere, an unmade bed, toilet paper scattered around—oh, and just for kicks, a dirty pair of underwear twirling on the ceiling fan. Now, look to the right: everything's immaculate. The bed's made to perfection, flowers adorn the nightstand, and all is right with the world.

This stark contrast? It's a vivid metaphor for the clutter and serenity within us. The mess?

That's the turmoil we navigate when our nerves run wild. The pristine half? That's the calm, the focus we gain through the STFU Method. It's not about ignoring the chaos but recognizing that we have the power to choose where we focus our energy. Do we dwell on the disorder, or do we seek peace and clarity? The choice is ours, and it starts with regulating our inner turmoil. Only then can we fully embrace the transformative power of the STFU Method, leading us not just to a quieter mind, but to a life where we're truly in control.

Alright, are you catching the vibes I'm putting down here? The chaos and calm, they're two sides of the same coin. Where your attention goes, that's the part that flourishes. It's not about turning a blind eye to the mess that needs tidying (especially if a spotless room is what you want). But here's the kicker, dealing with the clutter is one thing; how you handle it, that's where the magic—or mayhem—happens. So, when you're facing a mess, whether it's in your room or in your head, the deal is simple: tackle it, don't dwell on it. Where we often veer off course is by obsessing over what's wrong, instead of taking action and moving on. Let's not get trapped in a loop of complaints and inaction. Deal with what needs dealing, then pivot your focus to the pristine, to the progress. That shift is everything.

Our constant observation and discussion of 'what's not right' keeps these issues active in our energy field. This, by default, maintains their presence in our lives.

Some people confuse the STFU Method with ignoring issues and sweeping them under the rug. The STFU Method is not about repression, it's about mindfulness. I encourage people to be super proactive and handle quickly what needs to be handled, and after that...shut the fuck up. There is no need to propagate our lives with details about those things we don't want to experience anymore.

Once you have mastered meditation and started working with the STFU Method, you are ready to grow the habit of declaring how you want to see the world. Don't describe the world as it is. Declare how you want it to be. Give your life a second and wait until the physical world catches up with your intention, and it will get there. The more you use the STFU Method, the easier it is to stay positive and be more solution-driven. You won't talk about what you don't want anymore and will have more inner peace despite what is happening in your world.

It might seem counter intuitive, not sweating the small stuff—or the big stuff, for that matter. But imagine this: the less you cling to outcomes, the more life seems to flow in your favor. Crazy concept, isn't it? Let's dive deeper. Picture yourself desperate for something to pan out, say, a project. That desperation? It's cloaked in 'I need this' vibes, a classic case of scarcity mindset. You're convinced you need this win to be content. Flip the script, though. Embrace a 'could take it or leave it' attitude, and suddenly, things start lining up, almost effortlessly. Why? Because you've stepped into abundance territory. You're not chasing happiness in outcomes; you're already basking in it. You're not lacking anything; you've got it all.

Now I can hear everyone thinking, "That doesn't make sense. How can it be that the less you want something, the more likely you are to get it?" I know. It's counter intuitive to what we have been conditioned to believe. We instinctively operate to pursue things.

Think about it like this: if we had an inkling, a deep-down certainty, that the things we yearn for—be it love, family, a dream home, the career we've always wanted, or even that car that screams 'I've made it' (yep, touching on those quintessential LA dreams)—were already on their way to us, would we really spend so much time fretting over their absence? We're often caught in a loop, obsessing over our desires until they materialize. This relentless pursuit, this fixation on what we "need" to acquire, springs from a primal place within us, a survival instinct that's more about clinging to security than embracing the journey.

We lower our survival states by having a solid meditation practice (where we rewire fight-or-flight) and a strong STFU Method practice, where we "talk clean" and don't speak anything that we don't want to experience. The more we exercise these "muscles," the easier it gets... trust me! Before you know it, you will notice how things don't bother you anymore and how you think it's cute when someone is not doing what you want them to do. There is a whole new way of living when we lose the attachment to the outcome and the things we want. Ironically, the less we care, the more things go our way.

SIX

Lean Out Your Life

> **❝** *I'm a firm believer in new*
> *beginnings. Every day is a chance*
> *to start fresh, to be better than the day*
> *before. Embrace change, embrace*
> *growth, and never be afraid to start*
> *over."*

> *- Lindsay Lohan*

It has been said that the more stuff you get rid of, the more space you make for other things to come. This is a phenomenon that could be literal and also metaphorical. If everything is energy, and we often get rid of stuff, we are constantly making room for the universe and the unknown to bring new things to us.

This is not just limited to "things" but also people. There is such a strong conditioning that "the one with the most friends wins" universally, we associate "popularity" with success. From elementary to high school, we see this phenomenon: the desire to be seen and to be noticed.

There is nothing wrong with wanting to be seen or having many friends or a big family. The misconception is that we think that "the more the merrier," and that's not necessarily the case. The more we have, the more we need systems to keep it all together. This is not a bad thing, but something to consider.

I have always loved having a lot of friends around me, and I pride myself on being the funniest guy in the room. After both my parents transitioned out of this life, I became more of a recluse and began enjoying things that I never used to do, like having a Friday night at home alone or having brunch by myself. It was so powerful to venture into the unknown regarding different ways of enjoying my life.

I have stumbled upon a massive realization about friendships. Our days are packed with a finite number of hours, and within those hours, we're juggling countless tasks, passions, and yes, our relationships. Figuring out where to allocate our precious time becomes a real challenge. It's like we're constantly trying to solve a puzzle, determining which pieces—our friends and loved ones—fit into the day's limited space.

How do we know that it's time to part ways with people? They go away.   There are people we love dearly who have been with us for a while, and if someone dies, it is clearly a message that it is time for us to move on. And if we lose track of a friend or lose contact with them, it is also a message that it is time for all of us to move on. I don't mean to sound so "matter of fact," but once we process the emotion, this is what we are left with.

When we look at some longstanding friendships, we think that they should last for a lifetime, and some do. A lifetime for some could be one week, one year, ten years, or 25 years...and yet all these occurrences are lifetimes (they are "times" during "life."). A physical friendship with someone can end, but that doesn't mean that it's done. Look at it this way: what is the difference if someone dies or if you lose touch with them and you never talk to them again?

Then, ten years later, you hear that they have been killed, and then you feel that sadness, but in reality, they didn't physically exist in your world because you didn't see them or hear about them. It's when you find out that they died that you feel the sadness.

Not seeing someone in a long time and finding out someone has died is basically the same thing. Yes, the chances of seeing them physically when they are dead are slim to none (unless you go to a really good medium). Still, whether you see them again physically or not, they are always going to be in the only place they ever really were...in your heart.

This way of seeing people very much applies to friendships. Sometimes, friendships fade away. I used to struggle with this concept. I always felt that I needed to make time to see old friends and stay in touch with them. In fact, I remember that if I lost touch with someone for a long time, I would hold it against them in a weird way. I would feel as if I had been betrayed somehow if they had not kept in touch with me (even though I was doing the same thing by not keeping in touch with them). Or if I reached out to a friend, and they couldn't make time for me, I would be upset at them for not reciprocating.

Then, out of the blue, it hit me! What if the universe is orchestrating exactly who's meant to be in my orbit and who's not? Imagine, just imagine if we're meant to cross paths with precisely the right people, every hour, every day, throughout the year. What if the cosmos is subtly guiding us, highlighting who truly belongs in our narrative? Once this notion settled in me, my struggles melted away. I found a profound peace in embracing this idea, letting go of resistance and welcoming the flow of life's connections.

Recently, I parted ways with someone who is like a brother to me. This is someone I love dearly, but I started to notice that he would pivot in our conversations and begin complaining and telling secrets about other people. I really struggled with this one because he is someone I care for deeply and I know that he is trying his best spiritually and works on himself a lot. I even let him know a couple of times that I didn't want to talk negative about people and hear other people's secrets. This reassured me that I didn't want to tell him anything private of my own. Slowly we started to hang out less and less. I want to inject something here. I am not judging my friend for the conversations that he enjoys to have. I am just really clear on the kind of conversations that I want to be part of. Topics of conversations are like apples and oranges, you just have to figure out which ones vibe wtih you.

At the same time, this is where the STFU Method needs to be trusted. We must be careful not to fall into the gossip train. In other words, if I start telling people that I don't like to hang out with a friend because he gossips about other people, I am also essentially gossiping as well. Make sense?

I committed myself to not tell anyone that this person and I were not communicating. I didn't see the value in it. Initially, my primitive survival mechanism wanted to get people to agree with me, so I could feel justified for my actions. But I realized it would be more powerful for me to "be the change that I want to see in the world." If I want less gossip in my life, it needs to start with me. It didn't make sense to gossip about him in the name of ending gossip. Trust me, it was hard. When I hung out with our mutual friends, and they would ask me about him, I had to casually say, "I just haven't talked to him in a while; i've been busy." There was a part of me that wanted agreement from other people about my choice, but I wanted to take a stand to not assassinate his character by talking about him.

The other day I explained to a friend about how "I don't talk about the problems in my life" except for 1 person that I choose to tell it to. My friend came back to me and said: "But why should you repress and hold on to information by yourself, that's not fair." And I said that it's not repression, it's mindfulness. It's almost like if you have committed to a diet or a fast and you are meeting up with a friend, and he happens to be at a pizza party. You wouldn't go up to everyone at the pizza party and say: "Why shouldn't I be having some of this pizza, and you can, this is not fair. Why are you eating this and not me?" The STFU method keeps you intimate with your commitments. It destroys the seduction of the senses. It does take some will power to break out of the addictive patterns of complaining, gossiping and talking about the things that we don't want in our life. But little by little, with some will power your hard work will pay off and that magical transformation will occur. Just like you will lose weight from not eating the pizza and it will help you achieve your fitness goal, being mindful about your complaining will transform how you metabolize stress in your life. You will become the kind of person that as you are getting "what you don't want," you will know this is the best thing that could be happening. You will feel no resistance to life and every "No" will feel more like a "Yes."

I think we all have theories about why some friendships come to an end: people grow apart, they start dating someone new, they move away, and sometimes they even die. But I think people part with us because their time with us has been completed. I am not saying that there won't be another time when you come together because sometimes that happens, but the current time together has come to an end. And don't stress; maybe if they do come back into your life, it will be under different circumstances where you both will be more of an emotional match to each other.

I mean, we only have so much time in this life. We are all navigating through it and having different experiences. If you look at your life through a panoramic lens, your relationships will look clearer as to when and how they were supposed to happen.

There's something magical about holding onto childhood friends, those lifelong bonds that weather every storm. Yet, there's an equal beauty in meeting someone new and feeling an instant connection, as if your souls have been friends for lifetimes. Being woven into the fabric of a community brings its own kind of strength, but standing alone, embracing your individuality, carries its own powerful grace too. All scenarios are treasures in this journey of life, each offering unique lessons and joys.

Having any friction with someone is very powerful as it will show us those parts within ourselves that still need to be healed. That is why they trigger us because we are not healed yet. The people who trigger us the most are the real angels in our lives because they stand for our greatness and make sure we evolve.

Have you ever stumbled upon the tale of angels waiting for their turn in Heaven to go to Earth? It goes a bit like this: In the celestial realm, there's this profound pause before souls embark on their earthly journey. Imagine a gathering where these souls, these ethereal beings, share their earthly wishes. Picture this moment—one angel, poised to descend into life, voices a longing to know love in its most profound depths. Another, with a gentle raise of her hand, volunteers: "Let me be the one." She whispers, "I'll wound you so deeply that navigating through the pain will demand nothing but the purest form of love from you, towards both of us. That's where you'll find the most profound love imaginable." Doesn't that narrative resonate on some profound level?

If you think about it, it's the people who cause us pain that really help us evolve the most. There is a lot of enjoyment with a friend, but an enemy will make you grow and bring situations that will help you expand. An enemy will allow you to see your audacity, patterns, lack of compassion, and controlling ways.

To be able to look at our friendships that have come to completion and know that they ran their perfect course is the ultimate STFU method. In fact, there is no better place to be, than knowing and truly feeling that everyone gave it their best shot.

Having both of my parents transition out of this life was definitely the most painful gift I have ever received. And there isn't a moment where I don't see it as a gift, a painful one. They were both amazing parents who gave so many beautiful gifts to both my sister and me. Then, just like angels, they picked up and left.

One of the most surreal moments that I have ever experienced was when my dad was being intubated while he was dying of Leukemia. I was my dad's stem cell donor, but unfortunately, his body was already too fragile for the treatment to work. I will never forget the last time I saw my dad while he was conscious. I was with my stepmom and my sister. We were all surrounding my dad's hospital bed as the nurse was having him sign documents to allow for the hospital to intubate him. I still remember the whole scene like it was a movie. My dad was surrounded by family at that moment, but it didn't matter. This was a journey that he had to take all by himself. That moment transformed my life forever. In that instant, as sad as it was, it gave me the ultimate freedom to live. I no longer think my life will be less whole if I don't build a family. I used to think that the worst thing in life would be to die alone. But, in that instant, I realized that death is a journey we all have to take by ourselves. From that moment on, I have felt completely whole, whether with a partner or not. That's the last gift my dad gave me. He gave me the realization that wholeness is something I can have at any time.

I am very blessed to have realized that the biggest gift I have metabolized from the transition of my parents is that this world is not real. What I mean by that is that I can't smell my mom anymore, I can't see her and I can't touch her. I can watch some videos and look at the photos, but she is not here anymore. If that is not the biggest reminder that this world is not real, I don't know what is.

So, with all that said, life will lean everything out for you. And that's more than ok, it's perfect actually. Sometimes I feel that life is just one big preparation for death. We are born, and we have to let go of our youth, friends, parents, and, eventually, our lives. So, the whole experience of life turns out to be a great preparation for death, the ultimate letting go. As we prepare for this letting go, let's celebrate our friends, those who came and went (because they will all come and go). Let's pump up the volume on all the good times, the laughs and lower the volume on how things end. Let's honor all experiences as part of the divine, for how incredible they were. Life is truly a gift; let's be fully aware of that.

SEVEN

Shut Up! Literally

> ❝ *Success doesn't happen by chance.*
> *It's about staying focused, putting*
> *in the work consistently, and refusing*
> *to give up, no matter what challenges*
> *come your way."*
>
> *- Tarek El Moussa*

It was a beautiful Sunday afternoon and the perfect time to go to a BBQ with my friend Brian. I figured a cheap bottle of Chardonnay would be the perfect thing to show up with, and I knew just the right place to get it, my local 7-Eleven. I pulled into the parking lot and told

Brian, who was in my passenger seat, to wait five minutes while I ran in and out. He agreed (and by that, I mean he ignored me while he kept violently emailing on his iPhone).

I went into the store, found the cheap Chardonnay, and went straight to the cashier. And just before I got to the clerk, a little old lady bee-lined right in front of me, looked at the clerk, and said: "I think I have a coupon here for everything." And I was like: "FUCKKKKK." We've all been there.

What was supposed to be a five-minute errand was now going into 20 minutes. I couldn't believe it. It even got to the point where the little old lady and the clerk were debating over the color of a bottle she was buying. The clerk said: "I am just going to go to the back and make sure that the price is right." As she exited her station I just screamed: "I'll pay for the whole thing!" Everyone in the store looked at me like I was a crazy person. At that point it dawned on me that this was my moment to surrender. This was my spiritual practice. This wasn't happening "to me," this was happening "for me." I took a deep breath and just waited until it was my turn.

After I finally paid, 30 minutes had passed. I got into my car and Brian was still writing his email. He hadn't even noticed that I'd been gone for half an hour.

What do you think I wanted to do when I got in the car? I wanted to tell him about this little old lady who had bee-lined right in front of me and how I got stuck in a "30-minute ordeal" at my local 7-Eleven and blah, blah, blah.

But at that moment I had a huge revelation. Telling him the story would be like an addict doing a fix of drugs. My body was so addicted to the emotional rollercoaster that it wanted to re-live that situation and feel all those energizing but stressful chemicals all over again. But something inside of me knew that if I told him that story, I was just going to keep perpetuating my stress. I was meeting my complaining addiction face to face.

This time, instead, I decided to smile at my friend. I placed my right hand on the steering wheel, put the car into drive, and whispered: "Let's go." And just like that... at that moment, the emotional drug addict in me went to rehab instead of giving in to my addiction to complaining.

We have normalized complaining. Complaining is a cultural normality in our society. It's like we get a gold star in human interaction. There is nothing wrong with complaining per se, but...what if you knew for a fact that by complaining you get more of what you complain about? Would you still do it? By the way, this is not to say that if you go to a restaurant and you get the wrong meal served by your waiter, you don't tell him he got it wrong. This is different. Yes, express that you got the wrong order and change it by going to the right source. The kind of complaining that I am talking about is when you go around telling multiple people that you got the wrong order and that you always get the wrong order and on and on...

You are the observer. Quantum physics, the science of possibility and probability, teaches that through observation we put energy into things. When we observe things, they grow.

Now, I get it. We have to live a life where we don't only observe the things that we like or that we want to experience. There's nothing wrong with that. I am talking about the obsession that we have with reporting on things that we don't want. It's not so much that what we see is a problem. The problem is our constant attention and narration of what we don't want.

Let's take this out of the conceptual realm and let's put it on something that we can all universally agree we don't want to see in this world. Let's take on homelessness.

I personally work with the organization Hollywood Food Coalition and we feed the homeless community around the Los Angeles area. If I were to have constant thoughts of pity and conversations about how horrible the lives of these people are, it would be a huge disservice to me and to them.

The narrative that choose to tell myself is that (although this is far from an ideal condition) these people are trying their best. Thanks to them I get to have perspective on my own life and whatever I think is missing in it. Thanks to them I get to be my most selfless self, even if it's just for a couple of hours per week. I get to serve someone a meal who really needs it.

We could pretty much observe anything in life and give it the right narrative to lift us up, no matter what it is. Now, that doesn't mean that I am "pro-homelessness" or that I don't think that there is something fundamentally wrong when people don't have a roof over their heads. But, creating an empowering context over something that most of the world feels is the worst thing that could ever happen to them, is true power. Having the personal power to choose a narrative and not being a victim of our environment, in this case watching homelessness, is true freedom.

Let's go back to my earlier example of buying that cheap bottle of Chardonnay and the cute little old lady who got in front of me. We have all been in a situation where we had a clear idea of how something was going to be a quick trip and all of a sudden it became a much longer ordeal.

Had I told my friend Brian the story, it wouldn't have been such a horrible thing. But the insight that I got when I came back to the car was that I didn't want to relive that stressful situation again. By telling that story (putting energy behind that situation again) I was going to keep it energetically active so that it could happen again. It just wasn't worth it.

The human fascination with talking about what we don't want is rampant. Some would say that it's linked to our survival tendency. It's like, if I talk about that thing that I don't want to happen again, I am going to make sure it doesn't happen again. But the opposite happens. Talking about anything repeatedly keeps that energy alive. Then it's only a matter of time until that thing repeats itself. Sort of like when we keep talking about someone and then we see them. What if we are energetically attracting what we put our attention to? Wouldn't we want to only put attention on the things that we want more in our lives?

I know that a lot of people work in businesses that are about helping our fellow man and are constantly seeing things that they don't necessarily want to experience. That's when I refer again to the conversation about the empowering context. Choose the narrative you want to give to all of your experiences and welcome to a peaceful life.

EIGHT

Speak with Purpose

❚❚ *Living authentically is about staying true to yourself and not letting society's rules or what others expect of you hold you back. Be proud of who you are, show your true colors, and live your life boldly."*

- Stuart O'Keeffe

Diving deep into the STFU Method, you'll notice a curious shift: some people you hold close might gradually drift away. It's a stark realization, I know. Yet, in this process, a transformative energy emerges. Your appreciation for your surroundings intensifies, and you become acutely conscious of the energy you allow into your personal space. This isn't about loss; it's about refining your environment to resonate with your deepest values and finding peace in the presence that surrounds you.

Once the STFU Method really started to take over my life, some people started to fall out. These were some people that I loved and still love very dearly. People who do not vibrate with positive thoughts and constantly talk negatively will disappear from your life.

I had a close friend who would not stop talking about other people when we got together. The thing is, I addressed this with him a couple of times, and he didn't stop. Again, I am not in the game of trying to change people, I was more interested in figuring out if there was a place for this person in my life.

There was an amazing twist to this story. What I was failing to see is that I was creating who my friend was through my perception of him. By me judging him for being "negative or gossipping" I was locking in those particles for him to show up that way. Plus I was experiencing my lack of compassion and empathy in wanting him to be different (or even assuming that he had the capability to be different). I decided to just take a physical break from him for a while and just let the unknown unfold.

The moment that I released my grip on how he should be and how things should be between us, our paths converged once more. This time around I felt he had transformed. He was no longer the person who dwelt in negativity and rumors. It's fascinating, isn't it? How letting go not only liberated me but somehow opened the door for him to show up differently.

Start thinking of your words as spells (I have heard that the word "spelling" comes from the word "spells"). If you become more conscious of what you say, you will only speak about empowering things. You will see how your empowering words, your trust in the path, and the process will take over, and you will live the life of your dreams. It is a DONE deal! Your life is an amazing joy ride! You will become present to that.

NINE

Embrace the Unknown

> **❚❚** *Closing chapters of life isn't about forgetting the past, but rather embracing the lessons it taught us and moving forward with newfound wisdom and strength."*
>
> *- Brittny Gastineau*

My friend Sebastian just sent me an audio recording from Alan Watts. In case you aren't familiar with Alan Watts, he was an incredible spiritual teacher heavily influenced by

Buddhism. He talked about what is probably the biggest taboo subject in life...death. After both my parents passed away, death took on a pivotal role in my life. That role wasn't a depressing, looming one, but since I had no choice but to be with their death, I wanted to learn all I could and make the most of it.

I had a beautiful friend named Laraine who passed away from cancer a few years ago. Right before she died, she said, "No one will ever know how to live until they fully accept that they will die." I think most people approach life thinking that if they never speak about death, then maybe it will never come. It's almost like by not addressing death, someone will suddenly notice you're still around and say, "Hey! Aren't you like 120 years old?"

I really believe there is a correlation between mental illness and the disbelief of something more after this life. There is so much more to life than just getting a job, working out, taking care of your family, doing charity work, and all of the other social duties. What I mean is that if you don't believe that there is more than just this life, that's not good, because you know how it all ends.

By the way, I am not saying you should believe in anything in particular. I think all beliefs are perfect because they are yours. I am saying that if you truly believe that this life is all there is and that there is nothing after, of course, you will freak out when things are not "working out." And what does it mean to "work out?" Working out means hitting the metrics that are supposed to meet your belief system about what a successful life should look like.

Embracing the reality of our own mortality unlocks the door to a deeply fulfilling and serene life. Hear me out—I'm not trying to drag us down by obsessing over a somber topic. But let's face it, this journey...i't's all we've got. Imagine, just for a second, if tomorrow never came for you. Would you want your last moments clouded by frets over bills, the dream home you'll never be able to take with you, the youthfulness slipping away, or any of the material stuff that, in the end, stays here while you move on? The truth is, none of these "things" accompany us on the next adventure. So why not live fully, deeply, unburdened by the weight of the things that we can't hold onto forever.

I am not saying to be careless in this life. I don't know how much proof you need that this life is temporary and that we never know when our time will be up. Ironically, not taking life so seriously is what's going to make you succeed in life. None of us will make it out of here alive, no one! We need to start collectively celebrating death instead of demonizing it. Plenty of Eastern cultures celebrate death. My hope is that, little by little, the world will become less scared of it. Death is the most inevitable thing in the world. And it's a beautiful thing once we stop fighting its reality.

Now, while we are here, let's celebrate life. Be good to yourself, be good to your body, your neighbors, and the world. But make no mistake that when it's time to go, it's time to go. Living a life knowing that it's not eternal will help you not to take any moment for granted. When we believe that our human experience is finite, we will be kinder to everyone and everything.

I'll say it again: be good to yourself. Use the STFU Method and speak about what you want in your life. Keep your mouth shut about the things that you don't want. Don't pay over attention to the negative stuff in your life. If you follow these rules soon enough, you will see your life is a dream life.

TEN

You Control the Narrative

> ❚❚ *Life is a journey filled with twists and turns, but ultimately, we hold the pen to our own story. By taking control of our choices, attitudes, and actions, we pave the path to our own destiny."*

> *- Heather McDonald*

The STFU Method has so many incredible benefits once we start using it consistently.

Once this method cements in you, you will start noticing that you control the narrative with everything.

I am not saying that you will suddenly see your boss as an angel when you have repeatedly had conflicts with her for the past ten years. You have full permission to see her however you want mentally. The difference now is that you will be mindful and describe her in the way that you want her to be. In addition, when you have a conflict with your boss, you can pick one person and tell him or her about the situation. Tell them that they are the only person that is going to hear your complain. This will create a powerful bond between the two of you.

I am not saying to repress yourself, but do you really think that complaining about your boss to multiple people will make the situation go away? Or do you think it will strengthen and worsen the situation energetically? You guessed it right... it's the latter.

Again, don't go crazy; I am not telling you not to think about it. I am telling you not to say it out loud to anyone but that one person. Remember, always think of words as "spells." Think of "spelling." Words are way too powerful not to be taken seriously.

I once had a situation with a friend in which we parted ways. It was so powerful because I fully understood why this friend couldn't stay friends with me any longer. I really put myself in her shoes and completely understood. I didn't want to tell anyone about it, but I felt that this was something that I needed to tell one trusted person. I called a couple of people, but no one picked up their phone. Finally, one friend called me back, Carolina, and I told her. I prefaced the conversation by telling her I would only tell one person about this situation and that she was my chosen one. This created a powerful bond between my Carolina and me. I could feel that she was happy she was chosen to be my one person. It felt so good to have someone give me a safe space so that I could speak my mind. After I hung up, another friend called me back, and I told her that I already worked it out with another friend. All I needed was one person to walk me through this journey. I was good. I love that I was practicing what I preached and feeling the benefits of the STFU Method.

This goes back to how I told you that we are all addicted to our emotional states. Our bodies will always want to recalibrate to similar ways of feeling. The stress we feel in our lives has become adaptive, and we crave it unconsciously. So, this means that we will energetically attract the "people" in our lives to help us detonate similar emotional states.

Again, there is nothing wrong with this per se, but it keeps us stuck in patterns we may not like. Haven't you noticed that your issues with people repeat? Acknowledging these patterns is not enough to make them disappear. But the good news is that I have a simple solution that will work for you...

Shut the fuck up!!!! LOL... I am telling you it works. Please feel free to think that your boss is the devil incarnate. Just stop saying it out loud.

I hear you protesting, "But I need to let it out. I can't hold it in." Really, well, *how many times* do you need to let it out? When you "let it out," you are not solving the situation. You are basically getting a "fix" by talking about it to someone. Like any drug, once your "fix" is done, you will get a break for a couple of hours (metaphorically, it could be more), but then, before you know it, that boss situation comes up again, this time dressed up as your mother in-law, and you will experience the same emotion all over again.

As an experiment, just "shut up" any narrative that is not what you want to see about your boss. Try this and give it one week. You will not believe the miracles you will experience; it will be pure magic! If decisions have to be made regarding your boss, handle them, and don't talk about them to anyone except for that one person you have chosen.

ELEVEN

Speaking Clean

❚❚ *When we become more mindful of*
   our words, we gain power over our
reality. Every word we speak is a
reflection of our thoughts, beliefs, and
intentions, shaping the world we
experience."

- Dr. Joe Dispenza

Our culture has definitely found a tipping point when it comes to our physical health. We pretty much know everything we need to know about what foods to eat and what to stay away from. Even though new nutrition information will always make its way in, embracing a low-carb/high-protein diet is a widely accepted path to building muscle and shedding fat.

We have mastered the art of eating clean. But what about a habit that is just as important? What about *speaking* clean?

Recently, I caught up with a friend of mine, a fellow writer who is navigating the twists and turns of the entertainment world. He was buzzing with excitement over a major milestone —securing representation with one of those high-profile talent agencies that make Los Angeles the dream factory it is. As he shared the ins and outs of his new alliance, I sensed a familiar shift in the tide of our conversation, the moment where the initial glow dims and the "but" emerges. Sure enough, he segued into his reservations about Hollywood's habit for green lighting projects only when a marquee name is in the mix. We found common ground in understanding that, at its core, the entertainment sphere is a business. Star power, with its guaranteed audience draw, often becomes the crucial ingredient for a project to leap from script to screen.

There's nothing wrong with this conversation. If we had this exact conversation in front of ten other people in Los Angeles, they would all agree that this is how the industry works. But here is the problem...

As innocent and "factual" as this conversation seems, it could definitely be spoken "cleaner." What I mean by that is our exchange about the hurdles of the industry is going to keep those hurdles in place.

Remember, we have to start getting into the habit of narrating life as we want it to be, not like news reporters describing what we see. Even if the whole world talks about the very real hurdles of the industry, we need to speak clean about how we want things to be.

An alternative way to talk about the industry would be, "I love putting together projects in Los Angeles because it's like a fun scavenger hunt, making things come together. This is business of art and commerce, and my goal is to keep creating an amazing product and combine it with powerful ways to get the message out there. I want to make art that is seen by many so that it touches as many hearts and souls as it can. That's the kind of art I want to make."

How we narrate the stories of our lives will create new brain pathways, and subconsciously, we will start attracting all the things we want. Remember, the subconscious runs 95% of everything that happens to us. We want to actively speak clean, so we make a habit of creating possibilities in our lives.

As we keep the habit of speaking clean in our lives, we will rendezvous with people who can take our goals to the next level. Maybe your next-door neighbor will be a big film financier, and because you always bring in his garbage bins, he will fund your movies. You know what I mean. The possibilities are endless. Our dreams can come true if we are mindful about how we tell the stories of our lives. The STFU method won't make you silent but it will make you mindful. You will start challenging agreements that have kept you limited in the past. At first, this may not feel natural, but after a while, all the brain hacking will pay off.

TWELVE

Beef Up the Compassion

❚❚ *Compassion is the language of the*
   soul. It connects us to the heart of
another, reminding us of our shared
humanity and the power of love to heal
and uplift."

– Abraham Hicks

I was having lunch with my friend Matt the other day, and he told me that he feels his relationship with his mom is deteriorating. He finds his mom constantly asking him what he is doing, and he feels she is trying to spy on him. He is caught between feeling responsible for talking with her and frustrated about what she says.

When you begin the STFU Method, it will take a minute before everything becomes automatic. I swear you will get to a point where nothing will affect you (or things will affect you much less and for a shorter amount of time). But, in the meantime, beefing up the compassion is the ultimate hack.

When I say beef up on the compassion, I am just inviting you to consider that you will never know what is going on with anyone other than yourself. You don't know what genetics they came with (even if you are related to them). You don't know what trauma they are carrying. You don't know what coping skills they have. You don't know anything really. This alone should open you up to bring big compassion into any situation.

By beefing up compassion, you are not agreeing with what the person is doing or with what they are thinking. You are becoming intimate with the fact that you are not in their body, and you have no idea what they are going through. That's it! I think we often automatically want to make someone else wrong for what they are doing if we don't agree with it. But the more you use the STFU Method with mindfulness, the easier it will be to resist that habit.

I invite you to look at the science behind all this (whether you are into science or not). Let's think about technology for a second. If we look at the biggest reason technology is created, it's to simplify our lives and create efficiency. This means that we will get more done by working less! That is the purpose of technology. As time on this planet progresses, we seem to improve our technology in all different industries.

I remember a study from a few years back that said we have made more progress in the last 20 years than in the last 100 years. With the creation of computers and artificial intelligence (AI), we will see an even bigger jump in technology. AI allows us to be super effective by doing the work of thousands of people with one machine.

Consider that the human brain is the ultimate computer technology activator, not just because of what it can do creatively by imagining new things, but because of the very nature of how it operates. The brain has found a way to save energy and be more productive. The brain figured out how to recycle old thoughts by using less energy. The only problem is that most of the old thoughts it recycles are survival thoughts like the world is dangerous, life is unfair, and I am not good enough. By recycling old thoughts, the brain saves energy from creating new ones, essentially saving fuel. Since most of our thoughts are about survival, we are entertaining about 70,000 of them per day. There is nothing wrong with that per se, except that we are living our lives in a loop.

Our job (in my humble opinion) is to create the ultimate brain bio hack! What does this mean? We must lovingly force the brain to go through the uncomfortable growth of thinking different "non-survival thoughts." We must make these new thoughts the new normal for the brain.

Humans are born with survival instincts and desires. We are taught some as well. I remember, as a little kid, the dark petrified me. I would sleep on my mom's room floor because I was so scared of being in the dark alone. I also remember that I loved horror movies when I was little. So, I can't say for sure if I learned to be scared of the dark or if I came genetically wired with that fear. I believe that it was a mixture of both. I see this now with my 8-year-old niece. She is scared of the dark even though I know that my sister has been really careful not to show her scary movies. Nobody taught my niece to be scared of the dark; she came hard-wired with that. Could it be that we instinctively and genetically carry information that tells our cells that predators come out at night? You have to remember that it is likely that an ancestor of ours was eaten by a predator somewhere along the way. I know...so sad.

How do you bio hack the brain to think positive, non-survival thoughts? You give it the 1-2 punch. You saturate it with meditation that re-wires the survival mechanism, and you shut the fuck up!

By doing the latter, shut the fuck up, you are "putting in your hours at the gym" (so to speak) by flexing your willpower. It's like when you are on a diet, and everyone around you is eating pizza, and you turn it down and say, "Nah, I don't want any; I'm good." That's how powerful you will become. After a while, your brain will be super trained in the STFU Method since you have put your time into training. It has been said that it takes 10,000 hours to perfect a skill through practice. You don't need 10,000 hours of the STFU Method, but it does take some time to become automatic.

I have been practicing the STFU Method for some time now, and I will tell you, it's unbelievable how automatic it has become in keeping my nervous system at peace at all times, no matter what. The other day, I was at the airport, and I accidentally made a mistake and left the terminal walking, so I had to go through the security checkpoint again. I was talking on the phone with my sister and got distracted. I told her I needed to hang up to pay attention to what I was doing. I am still blown away by how quickly and automatically I went into solution mode without telling her what had just happened or adding any drama. I rapidly returned to the security line with no resistance. I know this is just a little silly story, but the real win here is that two amazing results came out of this situation simultaneously. First, there was no need to tell her something went wrong and add any possible stress to her. Second, I quickly went into the flow of solving the problem without making myself wrong, cursing the airport out, or condemming whoever designed the airport. The compounding effect of living a life in flow will add up, and before you know it, walking on water will be a no-brainer.

THIRTEEN

Enjoy the silence

❚❚ *I believe that the only way to truly break free from repeating patterns is through self-awareness and conscious choice. Recognize the patterns, learn from them, and actively choose a different path."*

- Lewis Howes

Now that you have learned the science behind the STFU Method, I hope you understand how important it is to follow it so that you do NOT repeat the past. If you want to get into a new reality, you have to think different thoughts.

You have to starve the brain from the verbal, energetic power of words you don't want to use. Think of yourself as a heroin addict. I am not kidding. In order for you to get your fix, you need two things... the heroin and the needle. Having the thought is the heroin and saying it out loud is the needle. If you use the STFU Method, you no longer have the needle, and you can't do the heroin. If you can't do the heroin, you will detox until finally you are off the drug and sober (from complaining).

In this scenario, our vice is the barrage of survival-oriented thoughts that trap us in the repetitive cycles of our existence—our looping realities. These thoughts manifest as beliefs like "Luck's never on my side," "It's a dangerous world out there," "My mom just doesn't hear me," or the crippling "I'm just not good enough." But imagine reaching a point where you're "clean" from these self-imposed constraints, where these limiting survival mantras no longer dictate your life's script. This isn't about finally snagging every desire on your wish list. It's something far more profound. You'll find yourself in a state of peace no matter what life throws your way. It's not about getting what you want but about wanting what you have (gulp). You will find contentment and purpose in every twist and turn of your journey.

FOURTEEN

Master Perception

❚❚ *Remember, it's not the events of our lives that shape us, but our beliefs as to what those events mean."*

- Tony Robbins

I was obsessed with wanting the powers to move matter when I was a little kid. I remember watching movies like *Escape from Which Mountain* and *Carrie,* and I always thought how amazing it would be to control matter with our minds. With the quantum field work that I've learned throughout my life, I have had incredible results manipulating matter through energy. Although haven't done it like in the movies, where you see the person looking at an object and moving it across the room...yet.

An old saying goes, "When you change how you look at things, the things you look at change." I very much believe in this. Since we are the observers, and this whole world exists through our beliefs, how about we start practicing observing it into what we want to see. Since time is a construct of the human condition, we are always in the eternal NOW. The past is gone, and the future doesn't exist...could it be that whether something happens right now or later, it's the same thing?

The other day, an Uber driver was taking me to the airport. He was a kind black man who moved to Los Angeles five years ago from Africa. He told me he thought Uber was taking advantage of the drivers by paying them less than half of what they charged the consumers. I listened to him and thought, "I wonder how I could share the STFU Method and still be generous with him by letting him tell the story." Since I have been practicing the STFU Method for a while, I have less of a knee-jerk reaction of being "the shut the fuck up police." Letting people be who they are is the ultimate expression of love and generosity.

As we chatted, he inquired about my roots, and I shared that I'm from Venezuela. Typically, mentioning Venezuela opens a floodgate of discussions about the nation's struggles, its dance with chaos, and the tumult of social and political storms. But this time, I decided to steer the narrative differently. Instead of echoing the shadows that often cloak conversations about my homeland, I highlighted its beauty, gently mentioning it's been years since my last visit. When he shifted the topic to the ex-president of Venezuela, often blamed for accelerating Venezuela's woes, I paused. I reflected for a moment (I had never done this before). My response was the following, "I see the last president as a manifestation of the country's long-standing challenges, a chapter in its complex story. How history views his role in Venezuela's journey, only time will tell."

I could tell that my answer touched the driver. I believe that he found a way to internalize his own immigration journey with this story. He asked me what religion I practiced, and I told him to shut the fuck up! (I am kidding) I just said that I watch what I say very carefully. I continued to tell him, "Some of the "worst" things that have happened to us all turned out to be the biggest blessings in hindsight 2020. Only when we look back with a panoramic lens do we see the cause and effect of any situation and how it all made sense for some purpose. I told him that none of us make it out of here alive, and we all need to inject gratitude into our amazing lives. No matter what we are going through, millions of people would kill to be in our shoes, and that's something that we must keep at the forefront of our minds. By not speaking about what we don't want in our lives, we start to marinate in the wonder of possibility and melt into an incredible sense of gratitude that we all possess inside us.

At the end of our ride, I thanked him for asking me about my thoughts about Venezuela. This was the first time I could verbalize it with kindness and sincerity. I know I trust the path of my life when it comes to my native country. My perception of Venezuela has changed, and now I need to let time catch up with my new perspective on the situation. I do not doubt that someday, I will experience Venezuela the way that I want it to be.

FIFTEEN

Living Our Beliefs

> **❝** *The origin of the word 'circumstance' in Latin literally means 'stand around.' So when we let circumstances dictate our experience of life, we are just standing around - bystanders to our lives instead of being the creator of it."*

- Jason Goldberg

What if I let you in on a little secret? The life you're living on the outside mirrors what you believe on the inside. Feeling a bit uneasy? Hold that thought, because, honestly, this insight is packed with optimism. Here's why it actually is fantastic news: I'm about to hand over the blueprint for genuinely transforming your life. And this isn't like those late-night infomercial that promise to revamp your existence. No, this is the real deal.

You don't need to understand where your patterns came from to change them (mic drop). In fact, I believe that memory is inventive, and who knows if what you remember really even happened? The good news is that it doesn't matter how you got here; the only thing that matters is where you want to go next.

I have created the perfect two-step plan. You meditate to rewire your belief patterns of thoughts, and then you shut the fuck up.

Many people put so much value on instant manifestation. They want everything to manifest in "real-time." I used to be that way, but not anymore. I completely lost that agenda once I understood that time is a human construct and it doesn't exist. For me now, wanting instant manifestation feels like rushing through the most delicious meal in the world.

Sure, a delicious meal is still delicious even if eaten super-fast. Still, I would rather enjoy it as a slow, delicious seven-course meal at a fancy French restaurant (especially if it's spread through some fabulous wine pairing).

One of my first personal development teachers was an amazing woman named Byron Katie, and she used to say, "There are only three things that human beings can really do. We stand, we sit, and we lie horizontally... that's it. What makes the difference is the story we tell ourselves while standing, sitting, or lying horizontally. I mean, if you are sitting in a million-dollar chair or a five-dollar chair, you are still just sitting, but the story of where you are sitting creates your experience."

 Consider that the first step to change your belief system is to make peace with your belief system. You truly are exactly where you are supposed to be at this moment, and that doesn't mean you will not be somewhere different tomorrow or even tonight. All you need is to first make peace with it right now.

Think about the beauty and grace of your belief system. You are this collective consciousness of a group of generational beliefs that came to you socially, culturally, and humanly. You have a set of core beliefs that most likely came from your parents. How freaking beautiful is that? You picked up the majority of your beliefs from the two people (sometimes one, sometimes biologically or not) in the world who literally made sure that you didn't die multiple times when you were a baby. I can't think of something more beautiful than that. Regardless of your relationship now with your parents, they were the ones who held you over and over again and kissed you when you were a baby. You became a beautiful being by picking up habits from how imperfectly perfect they were. I want you to be with that for one minute.

Now, you are on the precipice of your next chapter, a chapter where you get to thank them for the core beliefs you picked up from them. You have also found the freedom to create new ones. If that doesn't make you shut the fuck up, I don't know what will.

Life is such an incredible gift of perspective, and if you tune in to the amazingness of your being, you can feel at peace and in love with whatever life looks like in this moment. *Make peace with where you are.* If life doesn't feel great right now, make peace with it. Don't resist it. Watch what happens when you accept this moment for what it is. You might be pleasantly surprised by the miracle of the next moment.

SIXTEEN

The Law of Retraction

❚❚ *You need to be practical and implement patience, but you should also have crazy ambition. You need to have a 50-year lens."*

- Gary Vaynerchuk

We are all familiar with the law of attraction, right? Well, how about the law of retraction? The law of attraction states that we attract things energetically by thinking about them and saying them. So, wouldn't it make sense that we start *un*-attracting things we don't discuss?

I can hear you guys saying, "But how come I got into that car accident? I didn't attract that." First of all (stay with me on this one), are all car accidents a "bad thing?" I mean, Dr. Joe Dispenza had a car accident years ago that almost left him paralyzed, and that's how he transformed his life and became one of the biggest new thought leaders. He has literally helped heal millions of people with the teachings that his new path inspired. What about those who got their cars totaled and now have a new car? What about the people who got hurt and met the love of their lives in the hospital?

This goes back to what I said before, only in hindsight 20/20 can we see how all the "bad things" that happened to us were part of our story. Think about your life as the most delicious dish. Every experience that you've had has been an ingredient to this perfect recipe called your life. Would you actually risk changing the perfection of this dish by taking away one of the ingredients? Even if that ingredient was "painful" it lead you to where you are today.

Everything makes sense when we look at life with a panoramic lens. Consider that everything that is happening and has happened is part of the plan. If it happened, then it was necessary for you to go through that experience. At the same time, remember that you are the observer; if you stop observing something, it will most likely disappear. I am not saying to ignore it. By all means, handle your shit. But don't go around telling the world about things you don't want to happen to you again. Some situations that seem bad may appear in your life. They didn't appear because of karma or because God is punishing you. Consider that they are happening so that you can expand and free yourself from your environment dictating how you feel.

I recently returned from a retreat where the STFU Method was tested on me. The flight home went from being delayed for an hour, then two, then three, and finally, it was canceled until the next day. I was stranded at the airport. The whole experience felt so perfect to be happening right after this retreat.

What was mind-blowing for me was how calmly I handled the situation. I didn't immediately think about how unlucky I was. I actually thought about how lucky I was that this was happening *for* me. It was as if the universe was saying, "Ok, so you think you have this whole meditation retreat down pat? Why don't you put your money where your mouth is?" When I went to my hotel that the airline had booked me for that night (one-star hotel at best), I sat in my room and became overwhelmed with a sense of love and pride for myself. I got what I came to get out of that retreat, which was my emotional independence. I was no longer a victim of my environment to feel at peace. Sure, many of my friends who stayed an extra night at the retreat had a magical time reintegrating by having a nice dinner with the other people who stayed. On the other hand, I had to "face the music" of my life. But what a gift it was for me to experience the power of what I had learned in the retreat and put it into practice.

When you take on the knowledge that you are the observer, you discover that "observation" is an action. I am not saying you need to cover your eyes when you see something bad. I am saying something even more powerful. I am saying don't hide from the world. Observe it. You get to decide the meaning of what you are observing. If you see a homeless person, see a person who is trying their best effort to survive. If you see a war in the world, see the people involved as souls that are taking a bullet to raise human consciousness and evolution. You get to dictate whatever you want things to mean in the world. The law of retraction says that what you observe less often disappears. And if you must observe it, make it mean something kinder and compassionate for you and the world. It doesn't mean that you have to condone it. In fact, I encourage you to take quick action if you want to change something. Just move on from giving it energy and making the problem bigger. Just shut the fuck up.

SEVENTEEN

Stop Type Casting

❚❚ *Your beliefs are what creates your reality."*

- Oprah Winfrey

I believe it was Shakespeare who once wrote, "All the world is a stage and all the men and women merely players. They have their exits and their entrances. And one man in his time plays many parts."

This statement is as true today as it was hundreds of years ago. What if we are all actors in this so-called movie named *Life*? The good news is that if there is a character in your movie that you don't like, you could cut him out. Sure, if it's a friend that you are not getting along with, you could get rid of him. But what if the character in your movie is someone you can't eliminate, like a mother-in-law? (Again, I am sorry for picking mothers-in-law.)

You can't kill off a mother-in-law like a character in a bad soap opera. The reason she is here is to heal you. She is a central character in your movie, so you get the lesson/healing that you came here to get in this human experience.

You may rightfully choose to cut somebody out of your life or slowly faze them out... but what if there is another even better solution? Here is the thing: you are the observer, and this is your movie. All the characters follow your script's outline (how you look at them). I can just hear you saying, "But if someone is an asshole to me, how can I just choose to see them as someone nice? "Are they going to change magically?" A little work has to be done first, but believe me, this is doable. They are showing up this way in your life because you have some emotional addiction in your body. This allows them to show up in a way that bothers you. They push the right buttons, so you feel stressed out. Remember, we attract familiar feelings to ourselves (what we are addicted to). So, when someone is a certain way with us, we attract the perfect person who is spiking certain chemicals in our bodies, so we feel that familiar feeling of stress.

We are not doing any of this consciously. This is all happening subconsciously. I know it sounds crazy, but imagine that nightmare person at work; the whole office might agree that he is a nightmare. That person is only "occurring" that way because everyone in that office is craving a certain emotional, addictive feeling. So, how do you stop attracting difficult people like this? Well, this is your lucky day because I am about to give you the keys to the kingdom right here.

The are three steps:

1. **Start a meditation practice** - This is extremely important. You need to detoxify from your addiction to your emotions. People are showing up the way they are in your life because you are addicted to feeling like you do. Don't get scared by meditation. Start with just 5 minutes. You can find a free guided one on YouTube. This is the biggest game changer. You must give it a try. The meditation will get you ready for step two.

2. **Compassion** - Momentarily contemplate why this person is being a nightmare to you. Could it be that they are feeling insecure at this moment? Maybe they are hurting at home?

Have you ever heard of the saying "hurt people hurt people?" Could it be that they were raised with verbal abuse? Could it be that they genetically inherited it from their family? Could it be that they can't help being who they are? Will you ever be mad at a baby when he cries, or a dog when it barks, or a cat when it meows? What if everyone is doing what they are supposed to be doing? Beefing up on compassion is the first step to transforming how someone occurs in your life. Once you contemplate that the way they are has nothing to do with you, you get to break free and are ready for the final step.

3. **Shut the fuck up** - Stop complaining about this person. By complaining about this person, you are keeping their patterns alive in your life. That person is like a field of energetic particles floating in the air and when you call out "how they are," you lock in their particles. The good news is that step one and two will get you ready to shut the fuck up. And this is by far the action step that will piece everything together. When you shut the fuck up, you will suck the oxygen out of your addiction to this kind of person showing up in your life. Once you do that, the person will dramatically change, or they will exit your life.

If you have a problem with someone, I encourage you to address it with them, and not talk about it with anyone else. After a while of doing this work, you will notice that you don't even need to do that. That person will not be energetically aligned with you, so they will have to go away; it's just what naturally happens. I had a consistent issue with one friend because he constantly told me stories about others. I had planned for us to have a "sit down" so I could tell him how much it was bothering me. After doing the STFU Method for a while, I realized I didn't need to have this conversation with him. He just stopped the behavior, and I didn't have to do anything. It would have been fine to have the conversation with him "matter to matter," but instead of forcing my opinions on him, I surrendered. I just stopped trying to control him.

EIGHTEEN

The Matrix

❚❚ *Remember: The world is changed by your example, not by your opinion."*

- Tim Ferriss

We have all seen the movie *The Matrix*, right? Just in case you haven't, let me quickly recap it for you. Our main character, Neo, takes a red pill that shows him how his whole life is basically an illusion created by an insidious force that wants to keep people from seeing the reality of life. The reality is that none of this world is real and that the only way to get out of this fake reality is to dive into the hard-core truth. The movie *The Matrix* is an interpretive movie about our human life.

The word "matrix" itself means a hub or environment in which things are developed. To me, there is nothing evil or wrong with the matrix. The only problem I see with it is that we think it's *too real*.

What do I mean when I say the matrix is too real? Listen, we could all agree that we are given a name and an identity when we are born. We are told from day one (depending on what culture we are born into) what our destiny should be, what we should focus on, how we should focus on people, and what is right and wrong. We are told all these things without even questioning for a moment that they might not be true. Can we agree that our culture made most of this stuff up? You were given a name that was literally made up by your parents or at least your ancestors, and now the whole world agreed to call you by that name... it's that simple.

Navigating life according to the world's playbook is perfectly fine, but it sparks a curiosity in me. What if we could exist here, fully immersed, yet remain aware that we're not truly defined by this worldly experience? Is it possible to recognize that the many rules we follow are as constructed and arbitrary as the names we were given at birth?

I was talking to my sister Vanessa the other day, who is one of my greatest spiritual teachers. I told her that, in my opinion, one of the biggest contributors to mental illness is thinking that this world is too real. By that, I mean thinking that this is all there is and that there is nothing after this life. No one really knows for sure what happens after this life; I don't care who you are. But weirdly enough, believing that there is an afterlife is what keeps some of us sane in this life.

Our level of faith in the afterlife may be subconscious. If we really thought there was nothing after this life, we wouldn't act so carelessly (and I am including myself in that statement).

To me, reaching self-awareness or evolving consciousness means we can live in this world knowing that we are not from "it." So, yes, follow the rules and do life as well as you can, but always know in the back of your mind that this is not IT. Know that something way bigger than this life will happen once we transition out of this experience.

As my friend Laraine often remarked, "We can't truly live until we've accepted that we're going to die." Embracing the notion that this life isn't the end-all and believing in something beyond allows us to carry a lighter spirit. This perspective can transform how we view adversity; instead of seeing the world as collapsing around us, we approach life's challenges with a sense of ease. Imagine leading a life where, despite the circumstances, everything feels increasingly lighter.

By the way, this does not mean that breaking the law won't bring consequences. In fact, quite the opposite, you can freely and powerfully choose what you want to do as well as the consequences that will come. But, at the same time, they don't mean anything concretely. We create their meaning, too.

What I'm getting at is this: there's a graceful, serene way to navigate the matrix of life. It's about trusting the journey, understanding that every twist and turn is part of a greater plan. Embracing life with a light heart means we can face whatever comes our way with grace. Sure, not every moment is designed to be a blissful getaway, but imagine the power in welcoming each experience without pushing back, recognizing there's purpose in every challenge, even when it feels like everything's falling apart. How liberating it is to move through life with this kind of fearless acceptance, knowing there's wisdom in the winding road.

Awakening and raising your consciousness doesn't mean you have to leave your job, move to Bali, or do something super drastic. In fact, I think there is a way to live in the world and even be peaceful while everything is falling apart. Do you think that's possible? Have you ever heard of the saying, "Be in the eye of the hurricane?" Since I grew up in Miami, I have experienced many hurricanes in my lifetime, and while you are going through the eye of the hurricane, it is very peaceful. What if we commit ourselves to always being in the hurricane's eye? With enough re-wiring, we could all reach a level of peace in our minds, a peace that is so big and independent regardless of what is happening in the world right now.

NINETEEN

Trust

> ❚❚ *Trust your instincts. You know in your soul what's right for you."*

> *- Joe Rogan*

So, what is trust anyway? One of my greatest teachers, Byron Katie, had an amazing saying about what it means to trust someone. She said, "The ultimate *I trust you* is I trust that you are going to do what you are going to do despite what I think."

We associate trust with control. It almost seems that we are collapsing them. When people say, "I trust you," they are usually subjectively emitting a sense of control over a person or situation. They mean that they "trust" that things will play out the way they want them to.

Our addiction to control is deep and rampant in all aspects of our lives. Our survival mechanism is always trying to control and predict. The only way to lower the power of our controlling mechanism is through meditation, compassion, and STFU.

Look, consider yourself lucky that you are getting this information. You are getting the ultimate cliff notes/life hack so that you may enjoy "this life thing" so much more.

After you have been doing this work for a while, you will notice how much fun it is not to know things. You will have empty days on your calendars and canceled dinners; even being "stood up" will excite you immediately.

You'll be excited because you will "know" that something better is coming your way. Little by little, the dependence you used to have on predicting how life would turn out will powerfully lessen. You are going to fall in love with the "unknown." You will fall in love with not knowing what you will do next week, tomorrow, or even today, and that's ok. Remember: A "no" is simply a "yes" to something else. Trust that you are exactly where you are supposed to be and that every decision you have made has been the right one. Everything has led you here to this perfect moment. It's like your life is the most delicious dish in the world, and it needs to be made with all these ingredients called your experiences. Would you risk the life you have (being you) by taking away any of the ingredients and changing the recipe? Sit with that answer for a moment. I don't think so... right? Your life is the most exquisite dish in the world, and it took everything you have done to get you here. Enjoy it. It's a blessing and it is delicious.

TWENTY

Never Just a Little Pregnant

❝ *You and only you are responsible for what happens to you in your life. Nobody else. Not your mom, not your dad, not your friends, not your boss, not the president, not the media, nobody but you. You are responsible for what you make of your life."*

- *Mark Manson*

Isn't this just spot on? You are never just "a little pregnant"—it just doesn't work that way. It's black or white. Likewise, when it comes to believing in yourself as the architect of your reality, there's no in-between. You either embrace it or you don't. You can't cherry-pick what you've manifested. People love boasting about manifesting something incredible, but when things take a downturn, suddenly, it's a different story—they're quick to dodge responsibility for the outcome.

When I say something "bad" happened, this is also relative. I think we can all agree that every "hard" lesson in life was part of a powerful tapestry that ultimately brought a lot of growth.

Here's a tale reminiscent of one of my life mentors, Dr. Joe Dispenza. Picture this: he gets plowed over by a truck in a cycling mishap. Swearing to delve into the intricacies of the mind-body connection if he ever recovers, he makes a bold promise to the universe. Fast forward to a grueling six months of being bedridden, with nothing to do but lie there, face planted, envisioning the intricate reconstruction of his spine... and then, against all odds, he heals.

It's almost as if that accident was the catalyst that shaped him into the remarkable individual he is today. Dr. Joe Dispenza personally bears the responsibility of equipping countless individuals with the tools for healing. We're talking about thousands of lives transformed, thanks to his unwavering dedication. Some might even argue that he took a bullet for humanity, paving the way for countless others to thrive.

Embracing the role of creator in your own life holds immense power. I see Earth as this incredible school, where we're constantly presented with the lessons we've come here to learn. Now, let's be real—I think we'd all prefer those tough lessons to be a bit gentler, but more often than not, they come at us full force. It's like the universe starts off with a whisper, nudging us gently. But if we don't heed the message, it cranks up the volume, until it's blaring so loudly, we can't ignore it anymore.

I once had a remarkable life mentor who endured the heartbreaking loss of her ten-year-old daughter in a tragic car accident. Needless to say, her story was incredibly humbling. But what truly astounded me was her profound takeaway from such unimaginable grief. She shared, "A parent need not lose a child to grasp the essence of letting go. It's in those moments when someone cuts you off in traffic, and instead of reacting with anger, you respond with compassion—that's the place to learn the lesson of letting go. Don't let it escalate a bigger level." Take a moment to let that sink in. It's one of the most profound messages I've ever encountered. Life, with all its beauty and challenges, has this incredible capacity to humble us. The depth of humility with which she conveyed this lesson left a permanent mark on me. It's a message I'll carry with me always.

When you employ the STFU Method, you're essentially crafting a life by design. By consciously selecting the narrative you assign to the challenges that come your way, you reclaim your power. And that's just scratching the surface of its potential.

TWENTY-ONE

Navigate Algorithms

❚❚ *When we change our habits, we change our lives."*

- Gretchen Rubin

Have you heard people talk about how your phone is listening to everything you say? You offhandedly mentioned something about paper towels, and now, all of a sudden, you are being targeted with ads for paper towels on your Instagram.

Some people think that phones record our conversations so companies can market to us and tell us what to buy. Well, they could be right and...

As you get more accustomed to using the STFU Method, you'll notice something fascinating: your phone seems to anticipate your thoughts without you even needing to vocalize them. It's like the algorithm tunes into your mind, capturing whatever crosses your thoughts and bringing it into your reality.

You know, the deeper you dive into the STFU Method, the more you tap into life's enchantment. It's like plugging into a dimension beyond our regular senses—beyond what we can smell, touch, taste, see, or hear. Once you're plugged in, manifestations start flowing from this profoundly magical source. But here's the thing: with great manifestation comes great responsibility. You start realizing that the moment you think about something, it starts popping up in the material world, almost like a cosmic confirmation of your thoughts.

Embracing responsibility in your speech (and soon, your thoughts) will become second nature. That typical paranoia folks have about "Big Brother" listening? It transforms into a profound understanding that you've plugged into this unified field of intelligence. And let me tell you, the sense of connection you experience —it's pure magic.

We're stepping into an era where everything seems to be accelerating in the material realm. Technology is racing to keep pace with our thoughts—it's like a mirror reflecting the speed of our minds. But here's the kicker: it's a double-edged sword. Whether you believe life is fantastic or dreadful, that belief will manifest quicker than ever before. So, watch what you think—it's shaping your reality at warp speed.

Like I've mentioned earlier, here's the silver lining: the STFU Method will become a breeze for you. You'll find yourself naturally gravitating towards thoughts that resonate with your desires. Life will transform into this thrilling, delightful adventure, just waiting for you to explore.

It's very important to have a positive, healthy morning routine where you feel you are depositing good energy vibes into your life. I give myself about one hour from the moment I wake up to do a combination of journaling, meditating, writing, and affirmations. I know that not everyone has a full hour, so start with whatever you can. Even ten minutes is great. As your practice starts to gain momentum, you will see how the universe gives you more and more time.

Believe me when I say, life's about to become a whole lot more magical. With each application of the STFU Method, you'll find yourself tapping into emotional realms far beyond mere survival instincts. You'll resonate with sensations that transcend the ordinary five human senses. Once you start exploring these profound senses, the ones truly orchestrating your reality, get ready for an exhilarating rush of ecstasy and joy like nothing you've experienced before. And here's the kicker: while the traditional five senses take a backseat, you'll effortlessly revel in their pleasures without even giving them much thought.

TWENTY-TWO

Don't Fight for Your Limitations

❚❚ *Stay focused and stay dedicated, don't let anyone tell you what you're capable of."*

- Marie Forleo

One of the coolest aspects of the STFU Method is that once you get the hang of it and it starts running on autopilot, you'll notice just how much more mindful you become of the things you say about yourself. We tend to litter our lives with these casual negative remarks, almost without realizing the impact they carry.

If only we truly grasped the weighty cost of those comments, we'd never let them slip from our lips

When we (very innocently) say things like, "I just suck at math," "I am not good with planning," "I am not good at sports," or "I am not good with my finances," we are cementing these beliefs in our brains, and we perpetuate these limiting beliefs.

If we were to break down the order of occurrence of this phenomenon, it would go something like this: We have the belief, we think the thought, and then we finally say it. So, for example, "I am not good with money" is a belief. We think this about ourselves, and then we say it. We can reverse engineer this and follow the order backward, eventually killing this belief.

The next time you are in a situation where you are short of cash and that familiar feeling comes up, and you are about to say it out loud, take a breath and stop, STFU (don't say you are bad with money). When we stop verbalizing our thoughts, we will start sucking the life out of that belief, and it will eventually die. Meaning you will stop producing the thought. Like magic, the thought will disappear, never to be spoken about again. Ever!

The STFU Method will encourage you to stop fighting for your limitations. You will stop reinforcing the very things that you don't want in your life. The subconscious mind works by repetition, and the more we repeat a statement out loud, the more it is cemented, and it keeps proving itself to be true.

Initially, it might seem strange to break the habit of repeating those self-deprecating phrases you've carried with you for so long. But gradually, you'll begin to notice a profound shift as you essentially detoxify yourself from these toxic patterns. Step by step, you'll feel lighter, freer, and more empowered as you shed those harmful habits.

Look, if you genuinely believe you're incredible at everything you do, then by all means, hold onto that belief! What I'm coming after here are those pesky limiting beliefs we harbor about ourselves—the ones that hold us back from reaching our full potential, our true greatness. It's time to ditch those and embrace the boundless possibilities that await us.

TWENTY-THREE

Gratitude

> ❚❚ *Gratitude is the ultimate game changer, it can turn what we have into enough, and more."*
>
> *- Ed Mylett*

Believe it or not, gratitude is a huge part of the STFU Method. No negative thoughts are produced when you are in a state of gratitude. In fact, gratitude is the only "exception" to the STFU Method. You are encouraged to speak in gratitude as much as you want.

As per numerous new thought leaders, gratitude stands as the pinnacle of receiving.

Expressing heartfelt gratitude for every aspect of your life, without exception, signifies the ultimate state where manifestation truly flourishes. Saying "thank you" for the entirety of your existence unlocks the doors to boundless possibilities.

When you are in gratitude, you vibrate with the highest "wholeness." It's funny because we go around our lives wanting all these different things to happen. We want the relationship, the house in the hills, the great body, the family, the vacations, etc. But what we are really looking for is wholeness.

Let me break down what I mean by wholeness. Picture it like this: when we desire things, it's often because we feel a sense of lacking, like something is missing. We convince ourselves that happiness hinges on acquiring various external factors. But what if I told you there's another perspective? It's a place where desires stem not from a sense of lack, but from a deep-seated feeling of completeness, of wholeness within ourselves.

Living life with the understanding that we are already whole fundamentally shifts how we approach our desires—it's a win-win scenario. When we want things from this place of inner completeness, it's a win because if we attain them, they enhance the richness of our lives. And if we don't acquire them, we swiftly recognize that they weren't meant for us in the first place. It's a perspective that brings clarity and contentment, regardless of the outcome.

When we intensely desire something, we often find ourselves in a state of lack, implicitly suggesting that we require those things to improve our well-being. It's during these times that we become trapped in what I like to call the "matrix" of our own making. Consider the analogy from "The Matrix" movie: everyone was connected to a machine draining their vitality. Similarly, in our lives, it's our innocent yet imaginative minds that can deceive us. Our minds trick us into believing that acquiring everything we desire would bring us happiness and completeness.

There is nothing wrong with wanting things. Please, go ahead and *want* all you want. Just don't assume for one moment that getting what you want is really going to make you happy. Sure, it will momentarily fulfill you, but how long will it be before you want the next thing?

Now, let's tie this back to the STFU Method. Here's the connection: as you persist in monitoring your speech, you'll gradually detach from survival instincts and the dominance of the five senses—touch, hearing, smell, taste, and sight. It's not that these senses vanish; rather, you'll learn to place greater trust in the subtler, less tangible senses. I'm talking about intuition and inner knowing—they're just as valid as our physical senses, albeit less perceptible. Through the STFU Method, you'll learn to tune into these deeper senses and navigate life with a newfound clarity and intuition.

Let's ponder this: alongside our familiar human senses, there exist countless other senses, much like radio waves traversing through the air. While our bodies may not naturally perceive them, their existence is undeniable. Here's where the STFU Method comes into play —it serves as a bridge, connecting us to a vast array of these very real yet often overlooked senses. Through this practice, we open ourselves up to a whole new realm of perception and understanding, tapping into a rich tapestry of sensory experiences beyond our conventional human faculties.

As you relinquish the belief that our human senses are the sole arbiters of reality, a remarkable transformation unfolds. You'll find yourself becoming more intuitive, more attuned to the subtle rhythms of life. You'll evolve into someone who understands that just because something isn't visible to the naked eye doesn't mean it isn't on its way. Through this shift in perspective, you'll cultivate a profound trust in the unseen forces at work, guiding you toward the fulfillment of your desires.

Once you have mastered running your life by these invisible new senses, everything will feel richer and easier, and everything will make much more sense on your path. When "curve balls" come in, you won't ask, "Why me?" you will ask, "Why not me?" You will immediately understand that everything is happening to allow you to expand and grow. That is the beauty of life. From the right perspective, we will know everything is "for us."

The STFU Method will aid you in the journey of loving your life. Your language and your silence will describe the life of your dreams, your current life.

Gratitude acts as a powerful tuning fork, aligning you with the frequency of receivership. It serves as a potent reminder that you lack nothing and are complete just as you are. Immersed in gratitude, the desire for more dissipates, as you're enveloped in a profound sense of contentment. And here's the kicker: this state of profound gratitude becomes a magnet, drawing towards you an unstoppable torrent of blessings, cascading into your life like an unstoppable tsunami of abundance.

TWENTY-FOUR

Balance Your Communication

> ❚❚ *Allowing yourself to fully feel and express your emotions is the pathway to true liberation and self-discovery."*

> *- Brooke Castillo*

As the STFU Method starts to take over your life, you will be called upon to take on bigger lessons, believe me. Although your life will get simpler for you, you will also notice some incredible "curve balls" from left field. The powerful thing about these curve balls is that they will summon all your incredible newfound strengths. Your new way of being will be called upon and tested.

It's really important to understand that the STFU Method doesn't mean not speaking your truth. In fact, when life comes up, I invite you to confide in one person, or a couple more if needed. At the end of the day, whether you are aware of it or not, consciously or subconsciously, we want everyone to be happy. We all want everyone to be happy and at peace. I know this is bold, but before you go down that rabbit hole, just think, "How would everyone behave if they had peace inside?" Think about *that* world.

TWENTY-FIVE

We Are a Simulation

> ❚❚ *Life is but a dream, a fleeting*
> *moment in the vastness of eternity.*
> *Embrace the impermanence, live fully,*
> *love deeply."*
>
> *- Rich Roll*

When I was little, I loved going to the movies. I would go to the theater alone to see the movies I loved four or more times. The rich, vibrant colors on the screen fascinated me. I couldn't understand how the images were not coming from the wall but projected onto the screen. The idea of the projector didn't make sense to me.

I would think, "How could it be projected into the wall from the back of the room if I can't see the images also being projected through the air?" The images from the projector are distorted light particles until they hit matter (the wall), then they can be seen. The light particles can't be seen through the air before they hit the wall, but they are still there. And just like that, we arrive at an intriguing parallel to the human experience.

Consider this: we're like holographic projections emanating from a projector onto a wall. As real as we perceive ourselves to be in this projected reality, imagine the profound depth of reality experienced by the projector itself—the source from which we're being projected. It's a mind-bending concept that challenges our understanding of existence and the nature of reality.

Once the projection meets matter—our human realm—all aspects like our physical form, thoughts, and health fall into place. We essentially exist as a material projection from an unseen source, shaping our reality.

When you apply the STFU Method, you are helping re-wire all the information about who you are. This is why I say combining the STFU Method with meditation is perfect. Meditation will alleviate the knee-jerk reactions and addictions that we have to complaining and being negative. As I have mentioned, these are habits we have innocently picked up throughout our lives. These habits have been culturally reinforced and accepted as a natural way of being.

Consider the innocent habit of reading celebrity gossip. You wouldn't think twice about scrolling through Instagram and stopping at a post about some celebrity who cheated on their spouse. But, if you were scrolling through and the post was about *you* being caught in a cheating scandal, you would be devastated. I don't blame the gossip writer, the consumer reading it, or even the celebrity for being part of the scandal. I am pointing out how casually we are willing to look at something that would devastate us if we were on the other side. Do you see how insane that is?

We have normalized gossip to a state of relatedness and connection with people. We are stimulating and creating friendships over the misfortunes of others, and we think it's normal. I am in no way saying that I am "free" from this phenomenon. I just want to inject some common sense to the conversation.

The more you apply the STFU Method and meditate, the less you will desire to read about gossip or the misfortunes of others. Why, you ask? The thing about gossip is that it is a survival energy-based conversation. We gravitate toward it because we feel if we know something is going "wrong" with someone else, we will keep ourselves safe. This is all very innocently done through subconscious habits. It's the same reason we gravitate toward "bad news." We think that if we know what is going wrong in the world, we can keep ourselves safe by knowing where the danger is and avoiding it.

The combination of meditation and the STFU Method transforms your habits from the inside out. You go straight to the field where your projection is being made. You re-wire the information so that a new "you" is made. As you become more intentional about what you say and "speak clean," you will start experiencing life in a kinder way. Your level of compassion and empathy for yourself and others will go through the roof.

You will also stop antagonizing people. If you find yourself in conflict with someone, you will pause and think, "Who am I really mad at?

Their genetics? Their upbringing? The inherited guilt that probably came genetically from an ancestor?" The point is that finding the guilty person from this perspective is like peeling an onion. If you keep peeling an onion, you will end up with nothing.

I am not saying that you should condone any wrongdoing, but you will find a level of peace regardless of what's going on in the world. With the STFU Method, you will always find autonomy and peace in your environment.

I am giving you the keys to the kingdom here. Throughout life, we are taught to dive into things with our senses (sight, smell, touch, feel, taste, hearing). We have been taught to work hard and to really go for things by forcing and pushing. But what if we have it backwards? What if pushing and forcing leaves you depleted and exhausted in the end? Maybe you end up rich with a family, but you are exhausted, and then you realize that throughout your journey, you have been depleting your most priceless commodity...your time.

Across different cultures, the idea of hard work and perseverance is often instilled in us and revered. But what if there's another way? What if, instead of constantly pushing ourselves, we could achieve more with less effort? What if we shifted our focus to the power of our words and embraced the STFU Method? Imagine if we stopped reinforcing negative core beliefs like "life is tough," "nothing comes for free," or "things are always difficult." It might sound radical, but these beliefs often operate in the background, influencing our actions without us even realizing it.

One of the great gifts of the STFU Method is that you will become hyper-aware of your depleting core beliefs, and you will intentionally choose not to say them out loud. By not saying them you will start re-wiring who you are from the field, meaning you will transform from the inside out. By using the STFU Method, you will start operating less and less from survival. Your five senses won't control you anymore. You will trust life a lot more, and your levels of desperation and fear will plummet to the ground. The side effects that you will feel will be trust, love, security, internal peace, abundance, and wholeness.

I think, in the end, we are looking to feel whole. This makes so much sense to me. If you think about it, all that we pursue in life (and I mean all of it), from physical health, pleasure, a family, abundance, houses, cars, boats, and even helping our fellow man, is because we think that by having/doing this…we will be happier.

There is nothing wrong with pursuing all these three-dimensional goals, like the ones mentioned above, but what if *not*experiencing them could be even better? Now stay with me; what if you never built a family, but you built a life of travel and freedom? What if you never moved into that huge house in the Hollywood Hills, but lived in a studio apartment that brought you minimal upkeep and zero headaches? What if you experienced physical sickness, but also experienced the kindness and generosity of people helping you with your condition? The more I spend time in this rich life, the more I realize that the biggest hack to being happy is to fall in love with it exactly the way it is.

When I was little, I picked up the CD cover (and yes, I am fully aged now) of the singer Sinead O'Connor, and the album's name was "I Do Not Want What I Haven't Got." This is, by nature, a very Buddhist philosophy. The Buddhists believe that if you strip away all your desires, there won't be any suffering. I can see the logic behind that for sure. But I also love how the late mystical philosopher Alan Watts would debunk this and say that the mere desire to be desireless is also a desire. Meaning we can't escape the human game of wanting things. But I believe that when we practice the STFU Method, we start desiring things less compulsively. And I am living proof of that.

I think we will always have some amazing goals to pursue. The difference is that we will also not resist the moment "the way it is." The STFU Method will rewire our narrative about this specific moment in our life, and we will always see the glass half full.

No matter what this moment looks like, it is perfect the way it is. This doesn't mean you won't try to change it if you want something different. In fact, you can make it different from an unattached place where you won't suffer if it doesn't change. Transforming things when we are not in survival is a heavenly experience. You will be, as Abraham Hicks says, "Happy where I am and eager for more, perfect point of attraction.

TWENTY-SIX

Time is an Illusion

❚❚ *Time is an illusion, a construct of the mind. Live in the present moment, for that is where true existence lies."*

- Aubrey Marcus

When I say that time is an illusion, I don't mean that we are not affected by it. In our three-dimensional life that is run by the five senses, time is quite real. We use time to indicate and run the metrics of everything we do. It takes

365 days, 1 year, for planet Earth to travel around the sun. And we measure our lifetime by how many years we spend on planet Earth.

What I mean is that time only applies to the physical world. When we talk about the non-physical world, there is no time. Multiple realities that are not controlled by time could be happening simultaneously. When you are physical, it means that it will take a certain amount of time to go from one place to another; this is not the drill when there is no time and you don't have a physical body.

When we are very aware of our senses, time goes by really slowly, as we are surviving it. But when we are in flow and in the moment, it goes a lot faster. I know that we measure the reality of time by the wrinkles on our faces and the different 3D measurements, but keeping a healthy perspective about the reality of time will increase the quality of our lives.

The great teacher Tony Robbins says that time is a measurement of love. The reason why that seems true is because when you are loving what you are doing time goes by fast and when we don't, it feels very slow.

Maintaining a healthy perspective on time means acknowledging that it's a construct created by humans. In truth, there's no past or future—only the eternal present moment. We move from one moment of "now" to the next moment continuously. What's intriguing is that whether something occurs ten years from now or ten minutes from now, it's all happening in real time, because time itself is an illusion. While we might yearn for things to unfold instantly, there's great wisdom in trusting that they'll happen when the timing aligns perfectly.

When you apply the STFU Method, you will stop obsessing over time and find yourself flowing with the order of life. Consider this: if all the things you want fell into place right now, a great job, a certain relationship, a physical appearance, etc., what would you have? Just more "now" time.

The other day, I was at the gym doing my regular workout, and I started thinking of all these different projects that I am doing, how much I want them to happen, and how much happier I would be once they come into shape (no pun intended). But then my mind stopped, and I thought, but here I am in this perfect moment, feeling healthy, working out in a gym that I love on a beautiful, windy, sunny day on the beach. How much more do I need for this moment to be better? When we get caught up in these loops of life, I think it is because we let the automatic mind project those stories of how

much better life will be in another "now"
moment. I am telling you this with all the love
and truth in the world...this is as good as it will
get.

Listen, this moment, right here, right now—it's
all we truly have, guaranteed. Sure, your mind
might wander, imagining how much sweeter
things could be if circumstances were different.
But the truth is, there's no guarantee we'll ever
get another moment beyond this one. So why
not make the most of it, right now?

Saying time is fake is my way of saying that
past, present, and future are really just made
up. We are just constantly in the "now." The
more we can vibrate in the high states of peace
during the "now," the more we attract good
vibes.

Just a heads up: attracting good vibes doesn't
mean life won't throw some curveballs your
way. It all boils down to how you choose to
perceive the situation. Every challenge is a
chance for your best self to shine through. And
here's the kicker—your best self doesn't have to
fit any particular mold. The cool part is, if you
happen to miss one of those opportunities,
don't sweat it. Life has a way of dishing out
plenty more chances for you to step up and
show your stuff.

Life is an endless opportunity to be good in the "now," we just have to "sort ourselves out" and be good in this moment. Once we get into the momentum of being good in this moment, it will become easier and easier. Then, something will disrupt that flow, and we will have to start all over again. The good news is that this life is our story and narrative; if we apply the STFU Method, we will always end up in a good story. Not only that, as you narrate a good story for yourself, you will be inspired to narrate a good story for other people. You will also offer them love and wisdom about how they can narrate the right story for themselves. You will teach them how to apply the STFU Method to the lives of their dreams. Life doesn't need to be a "cold turkey" turn into positivity; it can very easily start as a gentle pivot into softly talking about how we want our life to be. And then, before you know it, it becomes your life.

TWENTY-SEVEN

Manifesting Power Through GAV

❚❚ *The secret to success is not found in the absence of fear, but in the courage to act in spite of it."*

- Brendon Burchard

As I have mentioned before, as the STFU Method keeps unfolding within your psyche, a lot of things will start shifting for you. You will operate less from the five senses (touch, smell, sight, taste, hearing) and more connected to fifth-dimensional senses like inner knowing, acceptance, and trust. As this is all going around, this is the perfect time to hit it with the GAV (gratitude, affirmation, and visualization). GAV is the fastest way to manifest.

Here is the thing: as you start flowing through life in a much less stressed state, things will start actually coming toward you instead of you fighting so hard to get them. It will be a "self-fulfilling prophecy." As you stop describing your life as "hard," you will have no option but to describe your life as easy. I really hope you are trying the STFU Method, even if just as an experiment to see if it works. After much studying the intentional manifestation phenomenon, I have concluded that combining the STFU Method with GAV is the way to go.

Remember, this practice is at its strongest very early in the morning when you wake up or at night right before you go to bed. This is because your brain will be in theta state, the state between wakefulness and sleep. This is when it is most susceptible to information.

When you wake up in the morning, grab your journal, which should be kept next to your bed. It should be titled GAV. This stands for:

Gratitude:

Write five things that you are grateful for. For example, I am grateful for my health, and I am grateful for my life.

Affirmations:

Write five things that you want to affirm about yourself. For example, I am prosperous, I am generous, I am kind.

Visualizations:

Write five things that you want to manifest in your life. For example, if my project is finishing this book, I write "book," and then I close my eyes and vividly see the book finished; I use all five senses to visualize a situation where the book will be done, such as being a guest on a talk show while on a book tour. Don't just visualize it in your mind. Really get into all the feelings of it. The great spiritual teacher Neville Goddard would say the secret is in the feeling.

After you finish all this, which shouldn't take more than seven minutes, meditate. How much time you meditate is up to you. I do anywhere from 15 minutes to one hour of guided meditation. While I am in my meditation, I think of my GAV and what I want as my intention for the day. My intention is usually to "fall in love with the unknown." At night, repeat GAV, except you don't have to do the meditation part unless you want to.

What I just listed above is the ultimate manifestation life hack. I swear that if you do this, you will see the magic unfold. But you have to be consistent. This is why I say to have the notebook next to your bed so you can see it first thing in the morning and at night. The subconscious mind will very innocently try to get you out of this routine because it is new. You have to be very intentional about this.

The STFU Method will be your manifestation enhancer. The more you use it, your resistance to following GAV will lessen. Your power to see and visualize your future will get easier and more vivid. You will keep affirming the life you want to experience, which already feels natural to you. Being in a state of gratitude is your biggest key. Being in gratitude will be easy and natural for you. You will be trained always to see the glass half full. Everything you do in your life will feel like a serendipitous flow. This will encourage you to keep going and keep dreaming big for your life. And to think that it all started with you just using the STFU Method.

TWENTY-EIGHT

Addicted to Worst Case Scenarios

❚❚ *In the end, we are our choices.*
Build yourself a great story."

- *Jeff Bezos*

There's nobody to point fingers at here. The way things unfold—whether it's a particular situation or a person's behavior—it's all just part of our human wiring. Why do we have a tendency to lean toward the worst-case scenario? It's hardwired into us, but it's also something we've reinforced over time.

I was on vacation last year, and a girl on the trip had her four-year-old son with us. The kid was not in her sight at some point, and I was next to her. I distinctly saw her eyes open up with panic out of nowhere when she realized she couldn't see where her son was. After five seconds, she saw her son playing in the other room. She calmed down, took a deep breath, and said, "Why do I have to think the worst-case scenario?" I never forgot her saying this.

Our brains are wired for survival, which often means preparing for the worst-case scenario. It's an innate mechanism designed to ensure our survival by anticipating and preparing for potential threats. This genetic wiring is present in all human beings, serving as a fundamental aspect of our evolutionary biology.

No matter where you live, we have access to so much news. News is an interesting subject. I see value in it, but the purpose of the news has definitely shifted. The news industry follows the protocol of a profit-making business model. I don't think they are purposely trying to torture us. But like any business, they are trying to be profitable.

Imagine you're the one responsible for purchasing advertising slots for Toyota commercials on CNN. Naturally, you'd take note that CNN sees the highest viewership during prime time. But what if you stumbled upon a spike in viewership during the Wednesday 2 o'clock news? Curious, you inquire innocently about the content aired during that slot, only to discover it's filled with stories of murder and war. You express to your CNN sales rep that you'd prefer to see consistent high viewership numbers throughout the day. And so, CNN adjusts its programming to cater to these preferences. It's not personal; it's simply a reflection of our innate survival instincts guiding our media consumption habits.

Stories that activate our stress hormones are the ones we watch the most. Why? Because subconsciously we think that if we know where the danger is, we will be safer. The problem is that the same watchdog-primitive system that is trying to protect us (fight-or-flight) is the same one that is making us so stressed out. By stressing us out, we are operating in a high-alert brain state (Beta), and that high brain state is the same one that brings down our immune system. This system protects against any diseases and contributes to the activation of our genetically predisposed diseases.

Using the STFU Method in your life will activate less and less of your fight-or-flight system. There will be a period where you will have to deliberately put in the effort (willpower) not to say the things you have been saying all your life. It's not only what you say, you will need to be mindful of what you watch and how you narrate your life in general.

Remember that you are the creator of your life by being the observer. I know this sounds too simplistic, but it's true. If you get anything out of this book, it should be to watch your words and be mindful. And if you add paying attention to the things you want... you win. This doesn't mean ignoring problems or not taking care of your life. On the contrary, when you apply the STFU Method, you will notice that your addiction to drama and problem conversations will stop. When life presents any "opportunities" (our new word for "problems"), you will handle them with ease.

TWENTY-NINE

The 3D World

> **❚❚** *Sometimes we're so obsessed with seeing the illusion, we forget to see the reality behind it."*
>
> *- Jay Shetty*

Alright, let's dive into this 3D stuff! Trust me, grasping this concept will make navigating life a whole lot smoother. So, here's the deal: we inhabit a three-dimensional world, which means we exist within physical matter, and it takes time for us to move around in space. We measure our lives based on how long it takes to go from point A to point B. And it's not just time that we quantify; we also perceive things subjectively with our eyes. In our three-dimensional reality, everything appears separate and distinct. And hey, there's nothing wrong with that—after all, we each have our own unique body, distinct from others around us.

When we're completely absorbed in this three-dimensional world, our five senses tend to dominate our perception. We become fixated on what we can see, hear, touch, taste, and smell. It's like we're living in a world where the motto is "I'll believe it when I see it." But if you want to become a master at manifesting your desires, you've got to flip the script.

If you adopt the mindset of an "I believe it and therefore I will see it" individual, you'll unlock the secret to manifesting your desires effortlessly. Before you know it, your wildest dreams will start materializing into reality. This concept is deeply rooted in the understanding that the quantum field is not just some abstract idea—it's a tangible reality. Remember, the quantum field is where all possibilities exist simultaneously. By believing in something before you see it, you're essentially programming the particles in the quantum field to manifest your desires into existence.

As you persist in practicing the STFU Method, you'll discover that accessing senses beyond the traditional five senses becomes increasingly effortless. These senses are intricately linked to the fifth-dimensional realm—an invisible world that profoundly influences the events unfolding in our lives. Did I lose you yet?   I'll dive deeper into this fascinating topic in the upcoming chapter.

THIRTY

You Need an Irritant

> ❚❚ *Adversity is not just a stumbling block; it's an opportunity to demonstrate resilience, creativity, and growth."*
>
> *- Andrew Huberman*

We all love diamonds, right? Well, maybe women love them more than men do. (No, that's not true. Diamonds can be a "boy's best friend," too.) Have you ever thought about the process a diamond goes through to be born? Diamonds are born when intense heat and pressure come together under the surface of the earth's mantle.

Diamonds need an irritant to be born (high pressure added to intense temperatures). We also need an irritant to be born (I mean that literally and figuratively). Our own diamond-like qualities will be conceived through the pressure that we feel in our lives.

It would be amazing if we built physical muscle by eating chocolate and watching Netflix all day, but that seemingly "wonderful" activity would eventually be the most toxic of them all. We all know by now that having a sedentary life leads to numerous health complications, such as high cholesterol and high blood pressure.

So, what actually leads us to physical health? A big part is the irritation of working up a sweat (whether at the gym or whatever we do for exercise). Taking part in a physical activity can feel uncomfortable at first, but its a crucial part in our physical health.

What I am trying to say is that an irritant is what ultimately makes us strong and healthy. At the same time, we need to balance out this irritant. And how do we balance it out? With the STFU Method.

As life forces us to navigate through its powerful waters, we will find incredible irritants along the way. Some of these irritants will be co-workers, our kids, our parents, our bosses, and even diseases. These irritants will demand that we expand and grow. They will demand that we observe them and give them attention. But, what is the story you will tell, when you observe them? Will you fall into the role of the victim and complain about how that irritant annoys you? Or will you lower the intensity of the story by injecting compassion and empathy.

When I say to inject compassion and empathy, it seems easier to do when the irritant you are dealing with is a person, but what do you do when the irritant is a disease or an unfortunate event? Look, it all comes down to our narrative about our lives. All I can say is that since I started applying the STFU Method, it's almost as if a dormant skill of "lowering the narrative" of my life started to take over.

When "bad" things happen in my life now (and I am using air quotes here because I don't really think anything is bad--its just another opportunity to scale my emotional independence), I pause and contemplate on what the opportunity could be. Maybe a sickness is telling me to slow down, or an "ending" shows a new beginning on the horizon.

I am not saying that we should repress our emotions and move forward without processing an upsetting event, but how long will it take to process it? I would never tell anyone to "just get over it," but I invite you to be mindful of your actions to process the situation. Are you telling only your therapist or best friend about it, or are you telling everyone who will listen?

For me, picking one person to vent to has made all the difference in the world. In fact, this is the STFU Commandment number two: pick one person to tell the story, and that's it. None of these commandments are meant to be used perfectly, but they will inject mindfulness into what you say. Once you start being mindful of what you say, there is no going back. It's like there is a crack on the wall, and it will only get bigger and bigger.

An irritant is what we want because they are like an exercise for our soul, making it generous, loving, empathetic, and kind. I know it may sound counterintuitive to want an irritant in your life, but trust me, a life of getting "everything we want" is a life built with no internal muscle. Remember the heart is a muscle and just like any muscle, when it breaks, it gets bigger.

I once heard an interview with Howard Schultz, the founder of Starbucks. The interviewer asked him about how he raises his children, considering he is one of the richest men in the world. Howard told the interviewer that he doesn't give them anything and makes them work for everything. The interviewer leaned in and asked again, "You don't give them anything...why?" Howard replied, "That's right. I don't give them anything because I don't want to rob them of the opportunity I once had." Howard Schultz came from nothing and built an empire. He knows that giving his kids everything they want would rob them of the opportunity he had. Howard built his life toolbox from scratch, and he wants his kids to have that opportunity as well.

When you apply the STFU Method, you will know how to manage your irritants properly. Irritants will become the ultimate factors for your success and your growth. Congratulations! You have unlocked the secret to emotional freedom and independence.

THIRTY-ONE

No Mistake in the Divine

❚❚ *Something very beautiful happens to people when their world has fallen apart: a humility, a nobility, a higher intelligence emerges at just the point when our knees hit the floor."*

- Marianne Williamson

Do you believe that everything is in perfect order? To truly believe in the divine, you have to believe everything is happening as it should. To truly be at peace in this world, you have to surrender 100%. You have to trust that what you have is better than what you wanted or thought you wanted to get. I know this is a hard one. Stick with me here, trust me.

Just a while back, I had plans to visit some friends in Uruguay. But, as luck would have it, I missed my connecting flight when I arrived in Buenos Aires bright and early at seven am that morning. Now, normally, this would've been a major hiccup. But thanks to my practice of the STFU Method and meditation, I had a different perspective. The moment I realized I missed my flight I just knew it was for the best. Instead of fretting, I called up my aunt, whom I hadn't seen in nine years who lives in Buenos Aires. I got to spend the day catching up with her. And that's not all—I also got to meet her daughter (my cousin) for the first time ever! As if that wasn't enough, I even squeezed in a quick lunch with my friend Isha, who I hadn't seen in over a year since she moved back to Buenos Aires. Talk about turning a missed flight into an unexpected adventure! As I was walking towards my gate at the end of the day to catch my flight to Uruguay I found myself crying. I was so moved by how the universe took care of me that day much better than I could have done it. My heart was exploding with love and trust for my life.

We need to start thinking of life like a GPS. We need to know where we want to go (in my example, Uruguay) and then let the incredible GPS of life dictate which way we get there. Some of life's most incredible experiences come from the most unexpected detours. I am a big believer in having a clear vision (or as clear as possible) but always making sure that you leave flexibility for the unknown to dictate the path.

Abraham Hicks, one of my great spiritual teachers, made this great comparison about life and being on vacation. If you look at a vacation objectively, you will end up in the place where you started (your home). Since you are already at the place where you are going to end up, why go? But then you remember that you are not taking the vacation to get it done. You are going on the vacation to experience a new place, for the people you will meet, for the food you will eat, etc. Trusting the twists and turns of life will lead you to the most incredible paths.

As you get versed in the STFU Method, you will experience those twists and turns and trust that what is happening is for the best. Maybe when you find out that you missed that flight, there will be a second when you will feel resistance, but it will be fleeting. As this becomes your way of life, as "life" happens for you, you will feel inspired to look for other options that have opened up because a door closed. You will know that immediately when something closes, another moment will open and take its place instead of lamenting why a seeming "opportunity" went away. Some of my greatest joys have been when I am in a seeming "breakdown" situation, and I notice how calm and collected I am in the middle of it. When I look back to a breakdown and notice how I handled it with peace and grace, I am usually moved to tears of gratitude for the experience.

You do this for a while, and you will become a master of reality, and you will easily and swiftly merge with life. Imagine a life where you know with 100% certainty that everything that is happening is for the best, as it is happening. No resistance, just flow... and plenty of STFU.

THIRTY-TWO

Wholeness in the Quantum

> **❝** *The idea of a multiverse sounds like an extraordinary new concept, but it could not be more ancient.* ❞

> *- Firas Elaridi*

As you develop a stronger grasp on your access to multiple possibilities and align yourself to the ones you want, some guidelines will be helpful. The STFU Method will be your biggest aid in aligning with the life of your dreams; this is how it works.

Since you will be a master of monitoring what you say, you will produce fewer defeating thoughts that would otherwise keep you away from your dreams. It is important to remember that you are the "observer" of your life, but observing is not a passive action. When you observe something, you will be much more intentional about what you *want* to see.

For example, if you see someone having some sort of tantrum at Starbucks, you will look at them with eyes of compassion. You will attempt to get into the world of empathy for their behavior. And if you can't figure out a way to feel empathy of why they might be acting that way, you will reach a level of unshakable acceptance. This means you will realize and accept that they are doing their best at that moment. You will understand from the deepest part of yourself that they are being who they are supposed to be at that moment. That doesn't mean you condone their behavior or that there won't be consequences. But it does mean you won't mentally go to war with what they are doing.

The STFU Method will be your biggest ally to find personal peace. At first, it will feel foreign. I am not going to lie; there will be a period when you will feel unfamiliar with the world and the strangeness of rewiring how you think and speak. Topics and conversations that used to bring you so much pleasure will not fulfill you anymore. Many people you used to hang out with will feel like strangers. But trust in your new actions and the unknown in general. Soon, you will feel so much peace inside you, and before you know it...a feeling of wholeness will be your new normal.

When I talk about wholeness, I'm referring to that sense of having everything you need right here, right now. It's a feeling of complete fulfillment, where there's no sense of lack whatsoever. This might seem like the strangest sensation, especially in a world where we're constantly conditioned to chase after the next big thing. But I believe there's a way to strike a healthy balance between embracing the excitement of the future while still honoring the richness of the present moment. After all, the now-moment is where true reality lies—the past and the future are just fleeting illusions. By honing your skills as an observer and fully immersing yourself in the present, you'll open yourself up to some truly incredible experiences.

When I say that the quantum field loves wholeness, I mean that the more you feel that you don't need anything, the more access you will have to the millions of possibilities out there for you. I know that it sounds like a paradox to say the least, but less you want something, the more likely you are to get it. But, it's true. What an amazing gift you are giving yourself with the STFU Method. You are detoxifying yourself from everything standing in the way of your dreams. You will feel the ripple effects of the STFU Method when you begin to notice how much you love you have for your life exactly the way it is. You will love how you look, how you feel, and exactly who is around you. Each moment will be a reminder of the miracle of life, and you will no longer take any moment for granted. You can be in the world's slowest traffic jam, but you will feel like you are at the best party.

As you delve deeper into the STFU Method, you'll find yourself embracing a profound sense of peace and wholeness. Suddenly, the urge to change your present circumstances will fade away, replaced by a deep recognition of your inherent greatness exactly as you are in this moment. You'll come to understand that greatness isn't some distant destination to strive for—it's the simple awareness of basking in the boundless sea of the present moment.

The quantum field will be open for you with its multitude of possibilities because you will feel 100% satisfied with your life. What if you felt 100% whole whether you got that thing you wanted or not? Imagine freely wanting to experience something without the attachment of believing that you would be happier if you got it.

Imagine what it would be like if 24 hours per day, seven days per week, you were 100% certain that what you get in life is the best thing for you. It will feel the same whether you get a "yes" or a "no" about something you want. And when you get a "no," you will understand within a very short period *why* it was the best thing that could have happened. Your brain will become a super effective machine constantly observing what is right in every situation. The observer in you will become addicted to noticing what is right and accepting every moment, no matter what it looks like.

The most powerful thing about this is that just because you accept every moment it doesn't mean that you don't also want it to change. You can accept the moment exactly the way it is while at the same time working toward the goal you want to experience. The only difference is that by accepting the moment now, you will get to your goals faster.

We have covered how time is a construct of our human life and how in the quantum world (where there are infinite possibilities), there is no time. As you feel more and more whole and complete (largely because you are no longer repeating your limiting beliefs), you will attract the incredible experiences you want. The best part is that those experiences will come, but they will feel like "no big deal" occurrences. That is another powerful side effect of the STFU Method: your level of pleasure won't be dictated so heavily by the senses. Yes, you will have preferences, but you won't sacrifice "the moment's perfection" exactly the way it is for anything. Listen, this moment could be all there is. Really think about it: we spend so much time thinking about the things that we want and rushing to get to the next moment, the next thing. How often have we heard those stories of people who never got to their next moment? Maybe there was an accident that took their life or some random illness that claimed them fast. Do you think they would have felt differently if they had known that day was their last day? What about every breath they took that day? Do you think they would have acknowledged it with gratitude? Really, what if this moment is IT.

THIRTY-THREE

From Wanting to Knowing

❚❚ *I think it is possible for ordinary*
   people to choose to be
extraordinary."

- Elon Musk

When we're heavily reliant on our five senses, the desire for something often blinds us. We see this vividly in children throwing tantrums when they can't have what they want. It's a natural part of human behavior, nothing to fault. However, as the STFU Method takes root within you, a shift occurs—from "wanting" to "knowing."

Transitioning from wanting to knowing signifies a shift away from the dominance of our five senses over our being. You'll still pursue your desires, but with a deep inner knowing that the perfect situation is already available to you in the present moment. Consider this: on a subconscious level, you might already want what you have. Think about it—when your reality aligns with your desires, that's when you often feel the most content. So, what if you lived in a perpetual state of wanting what you have? Whether it's sunny or raining, whether you miss a flight or not—it's all perfect, exactly the way it should be.

Isn't it fascinating to consider that if you consistently lived in a state of "wanting what you have," you'd eventually realize that you possess everything you need in every moment. Picture it—existing in a perpetual state of heightened wholeness as you navigate through life. In this state, it would seem entirely natural for your desires to effortlessly manifest, as you're already deeply content with what you currently have.

It's crucial to give ourselves a reality check from time to time, to truly immerse ourselves in the mindfulness of the moment. We need to pause and ask: "What does this moment feel like? Do I believe that something else could enhance it? What magical addition could make it even better?" And here's the thing—can we truly trust our minds when they suggest that this moment would be improved by something else? How can we know that it is true?

When using the STFU Method, you can train your moments to transition from a mindset of wanting to a mindset of knowing. In this state, you can still pursue your interests, goals, and dreams, all while surrendering to the certainty that the best outcome is always unfolding in real time. Now, I get it—this might sound a bit perplexing. How can one be completely surrendered to the present moment while actively working to change it? Here's the deal: the more deeply you immerse yourself in the STFU Method, the less you'll rely on your five senses. Pair that with meditation, and you've got the winning combination. Meditation will help you tap into higher levels of peace and balance, while the STFU Method will train you to avoid self-sabotage by monitoring the language you use.

To go from wanting to knowing will come very easily when you do the work. Before you know it, you will experience the most perfect moments and notice that you do not want them to change. You will move from perfect moment to perfect moment. Sure, there will be things about the future you will be excited about, but you will not want them to come rushing in and take away the perfection of the current moment. Imagine a life where you pursue and experience things not just to get them done, but from a place of complete surrender and presence.

THIRTY-FOUR

STFU is Your New GPS

> **"** *Patterns come from stories in your mind. Take control. Silence the mind to break any pattern."*

> *- Megan Pormer*

It's often said that everything begins with a thought. After all, the mind's primary function is to think. The types of thoughts we generate are influenced by our lifelong conditioning and genetic predispositions. Did you know that on average, we have around 70,000 thoughts per day? And as we've discussed earlier, many of these thoughts are recycled by the brain. Why? Well, the brain operates as a highly efficient system, recycling thoughts to conserve energy and optimize effectiveness.

This is where the brilliance of the STFU Method truly shines. You're essentially hacking into your brain's operating system in real time. By consciously interrupting the usual patterns of your self-talk, you're compelling your brain to generate new thoughts. Think of it like being your own GPS system, deciding to take a different turn and embark on a whole new adventure. With the STFU Method, you directly influence your thoughts, actions, and emotions. By refraining from indulging in your typical negative self-talk, you're effectively hijacking the brain's autopilot and steering it toward creating fresh perspectives. These new thoughts lead to new actions, which in turn elicit new, more positive emotions. It's a powerful cycle of transformation that ultimately leads to more favorable outcomes.

Trust me, it's just like any other practice. The more you do it, the more your subconscious mind will integrate it and turn it into a habit. Initially, when you start monitoring yourself and consciously focus only on discussing what you want, your brain will adapt to this new pattern. Before you realize it, you'll naturally gravitate towards conversations and topics that uplift you and make you feel good. Of course, you'll still be engaged in society and able to discuss current events, but you'll find yourself effortlessly moving in and out of those conversations, without getting stuck in draining or negative dialogues.

Again, this is not about suppressing any kind of emotion and not being self-expressed. This is just a level of mindfulness about what you say that will profoundly impact the quality of your life. Once you start to live this way, there will be no turning back, and you will love it. And, of course, this is not about perfection either. If moments come when you engage in gossip or negative self-talk, that's ok too. You will recognize it and keep moving forward.

I am a real stickler about having a powerful morning routine. For me, the morning is crucial in setting up my day. Grab your journal by your bed and start with your GAV (gratitude, affirmation, and visualization), create your intention for the day, and then move into your meditation practice.

When you return home in the evening, just before bedtime, pick up your notebook again and engage in your Gratitude-Affirmation-Visualization (GAV) practice, followed by a brief meditation if possible. Trust me, it becomes easier and more natural with time. You just need to adopt a mindset where, alongside taking action in your life, you also prioritize working with the energy field to align yourself for the day ahead. Keep in mind that your brain is most receptive to suggestions right before bed and upon waking up. Make the most of this incredible computer—the brain—to manifest the life of your dreams.

Remember, your dream life isn't solely determined by what you attain or accomplish; it's about how you experience each moment, regardless of its nature. By consistently setting yourself up right in the present moment, you'll cultivate a continuous sense of support throughout the day. You'll find yourself experiencing a slice of heaven on Earth, regardless of external circumstances.

THIRTY–FIVE

The First Act of War is Defense

❚❚ *Once you realize that everyone is right, there's nothing left to defend. It's not about being right; it's about understanding."*

- Tom Bilyeu

As the STFU Method keeps evolving in you, your desire to defend anything will shrink massively. The thing about defense is that it is highly triggered by survival emotions. These emotions are the ones that guide us to protect and defend. With the STFU Method, you will find less and less the need to control and defend; you will see that what is happening now is what you really want, and trying to control it would be like not tasting an amazing dish made especially for you.

The other day, I was with a friend, and we went to watch the sunset on the beach. He accidentally got his car stuck in the sand. We were in this vibration of nothing can ruin the moment. But two hours passed, and I could feel myself getting a bit anxious. But this was nothing in comparison to how I used to feel. We called a tow truck, and we waited. Finally, my friend saw someone driving he knew who gave us a ride to the party we were planning to go to after the beach. The tow truck never came, but while we were at the party, I had the idea to call the house manager at the place where I was staying at and asked him if he had some rope to pull the car. He agreed to come out. At first, the car didn't really move out of the sand, but after a good push, we finally got it un stuck.

Originally when the car got stuck in the sand, it was my moment to put my STFU Method into action. Since I didn't get triggered I wasn't reliant on my survival instincts, I tapped into my creativity and decided to call the house manager later on for assistance. And you know what? In the end, I even had the creativity to give the car that final push that saved the day and got it out of the sand. It was incredibly satisfying to go to sleep that night, knowing that I conquered both myself and the situation. I had a blast at the party, and lent a helping hand to a friend with my innovative ideas.

Life becomes significantly smoother when you commit to doing the inner work, whatever form that may look for you. The key is to establish a morning and evening routine that includes GAV (gratitude, affirmation, and visualization), along with meditation and applying the STFU Method. Think of it like planting seeds in your personal garden. Initially, your routines may not feel particularly thrilling, much like tending to baby seeds. But, with consistent care and dedication, those seeds will eventually flourish into a bountiful harvest. Before you know it, your garden will be teeming with sturdy bamboo, resilient and unstoppable. Your thoughts will become fortified, resonating with elevated levels of love and positivity.

When you operate from a place of high love vibrations, there's no need to defend anything because you're not threatened by external forces. Picture yourself effortlessly flowing with the currents of life without the need to force change. Change remains inevitable, but the difference lies in how you approach it—without self-criticism or the urge to manipulate outcomes, youou'll find yourself navigating life by simply setting intentions, without feeling compelled to take forceful action. Jobs, relationships, health, friendships—everything falls into perfect alignment. You'll be amazed by how effortlessly your dreams manifest, requiring minimal physical effort yet yielding extraordinary results.

THIRTY-SIX

Who Are You Mad At

❚❚ *Our perception of others is a reflection of ourselves. When we change the way we look at people, the people we look at change."*

- Mastin Kipp

After consistently applying the STFU Method, you'll undergo a profound transformation. Research indicates that the cells in your body continuously replicate themselves, with certain cells, organs, and systems completely renewing in a matter of months. Similarly, the changes brought about by the STFU Method will occur at an accelerated pace, reshaping your mindset and outlook on life in a remarkably swift manner.

You will no longer feel the urge to discuss any kind of drama, and you won't want to talk about things you don't want in your life. I went to a New Year's Eve party recently with some friends, and there were moments throughout the night when I was pulled into different directions to "sort out a little bits of drama." I was happy I could fully embrace peace while helping my friend. But what happened the next day was pretty perfect, too...

I don't know about you, but with my friends in the past, the day after a party is usually when everyone calls each other and talks about everything that went wild. Essentially everyone shares all the gossip and the good stories. The day after that New Year's Eve party, I had zero desire to discuss anything related to the drama of the night before. I wasn't sure who knew what, but it didn't matter.

I can't begin to tell you how satisfying it feels to know I overcame old ways of being. It felt so good to show up as someone who just spreads peace, lends an ear, lends a hand and offers solutions. I feel so humbled because my default setting has become to lend an ear and a hand to anyone who needs a sounding board.

As I mentioned before, with the STFU Method, everyone gets a pass. Remember to ask yourself, "Who am I really mad at?" When someone upsets you, I want you to identify the real enemy (in your eyes). Can't find the enemy? That's because it doesn't exist. Stay with me.

When we are in conflict, the only real enemy is how we think about it. Your enemy will disappear when you sort out your thoughts about a situation.

In the most basic of terms, when you are mad at anything or anyone, you just resist it being the way it is. You are fighting with reality. This is not to say that what you are mad at will not eventually change or that you shouldn't stay away from it. When you are experiencing something that you don't enjoy (whether it's a person or a movie that is annoying you), get real with yourself about why you chose to be there. Maybe you are helping out a friend and think that if you were in their situation, you would want someone to have your back. Whatever it is, you get to pick the story that sorts you out. What I mean by this is that we all have the power to choose a narrative about any situation that we are in, to make the situation bearable if we are not necessarily enjoying it.

When I question who I am mad at, it makes the upset fade away. As you become more and more intimate with the STFU Method, you will grow to accept how things are. The irony is that by accepting the way things are, things will start going your way because you will not be in resistance. The energy of resistance brings more resistance, but the energy of flow aligns with more flow.

What fun it is to be *in* this world but not be *of* it and to know that whatever wiring we came with can be re-wired. When I speak of the STFU Method, I am inviting you to speak up for the life of your dreams.

THIRTY-SEVEN

Truth, Kindness and the Benefit

❚❚ *Life is not about finding yourself,*
it's about creating yourself."

- Steven Bartlett

So much of this book is credited to my best friend, Kelly Sprague, who is an incredible teacher and new thought leader. Kelly has been both a student and teacher of spirituality for most of her life, and her mere presence can touch your heart. I have been telling Kelly for a while now, "If I ever write a spiritual book, it will be called the STFU Method!" Finally, one day, Kelly challenged me, "When are you going to start writing this book?" and voilà, here it is!

She once told me that before she joins in a conversation, she has three questions in mind, "Is it true? Is it kind? And is it beneficial to the other person?" I feel these are amazing rule-of-thumb questions to ask before engaging in any conversation. Remember that the STFU Method will become more automatic as you go deep into the practice, and until you get there, you just have to be intentional about what you say.

Of course, there are moments when you will gossip or not speak highly about someone in particular. And that's ok. The fact that you will now be mindful of what you say will make all the difference in the world for you.

There is no right or wrong way to use the STFU Method. I know this may sound strange, but trust me. Once you become more mindful, you will notice how little you talk about the things and people you don't want to experience.

I want you to pay close attention to what I just wrote. I really want it to land here. When you say negative things about someone, you're really just describing someone you don't want to experience. This doesn't mean you have to keep them in your life, but your experiences with them will probably match the negative things you've said. In another way, your words can affect how you see and interact with people. If you say someone is "a pain in the ass," you feed energy into keeping that person a pain in the ass in your experience. If someone tells you, "Bobby is a nightmare," and you reply with, "Well, he is interesting," you will see how your new verbal creation of that person will start transforming your experience with him.

I get really excited when I meet someone that I don't like. I think, "What story am I telling myself about you that keeps me away from enjoying you?" I don't care how many people think Bobby is a nightmare; the minute I agree, I'm the one who loses. And then the question becomes, "Do you want to be right, or do you want to be happy?" If you want to be right, go ahead and agree with the majority of people calling Bobby a nightmare. But if you want to be happy, commit yourself to being wrong about Bobby.

Find that compassionate characteristic in the person you might otherwise talk negatively about. Look for something that can help you see them more empathetically. The minute you apply empathy to someone, you have allowed yourself to experience that person differently.

Remember, this whole world exists in your interpretation of it. Everything! Clean up how you see everyone and watch the magic unfold. When I say clean up, I mean that if someone shows up aggressive in your life, start wondering how they got that way and soften that narrative. And yet, still do what you must, whether that means leaving or telling that person their behavior is not sitting well with you.

Through my journey with the STFU Method, I discovered a remarkable phenomenon: I no longer felt compelled to confront others about their behaviors or traits that didn't resonate with me. Instead, I focused on internalizing the work and shaping my perceptions of them in alignment with my desires. Astonishingly, I witnessed how individuals either underwent positive changes or naturally drifted away from my life. This process of transformation is cumulative; as the saying goes, "you are where you are." By consistently applying the method, I gradually reaped the benefits, experiencing incremental improvements in my life.

The beauty of the STFU Method lies in its simplicity and profound effectiveness. By embracing the principle of "describe the world how you want it to be and see it that way," you empower yourself to shape your reality according to your desires. Through the practice of silencing negative self-talk and consciously framing your perceptions, you pave the way toward manifesting the life of your dreams.

Before you enter a conversation, remember to ask yourself, "Is it true? Is it kind? Is it beneficial to the other person?" Kelly gave me this great tool, and now I am giving it to you. The more you use this, the more it will become innate and automatic in you. Before you know it, you will go from miracle conversation to miracle conversation. You will live in awe of how much you love everyone and how much they love you.

THIRTY-EIGHT

Overcome Your Environment

❚❚ *We are not imprisoned by our*
circumstances. We are freed by our
choices."

- Ryan Holiday

This topic is peppered, if not marinated, throughout this book. I have lived in Los Angeles for the past 2 decades, and I remember right before I moved from New York, everyone told me that I would hate LA and that I would be back in no time. When people said that, in my head, I would say, "Thank you for sharing, but that's not going to be my experience."

Or so I thought.

My first experience in LA was as a photography agent. I represented photographers and produced photo shoots.

Soon after I arrived, I landed in a celebrity circle of friends. I became friends with a celebrity photographer and his celebrity muse. One day, they invited me to a Hollywood party. Let's just say that the host was thrilled when we showed up. I am not going to lie; this was the best treatment I have ever had. He was gushing all over all three of us equally. At that moment, I could clearly see how being a celebrity was addictive. Who wouldn't love to be adored like that? The host told me the party would last all week, and that I was more than welcome to return the next day.

So, of course, I came back the next day. But this time, I brought two "non-celebrity" photographers I represented. As soon as I walked in through the door, I ran into the host of the party. He didn't even look at me. I am not kidding. I put myself right in front of him, and it was like had never met me in his entire life. I tried to playfully grab him, and he whisked my hand away.

At that moment, I remember vividly becoming infused with rage. It was almost as if time stopped. All I could hear at that moment were the voices of my friends from New York telling me that everyone in LA was so fake and "Hollywood this..." and "Hollywood that..."

But then my rage halted, a huge download came down on me. I heard a god like voice say, "It's not personal."

A wave of peace washed over all me. Peace took complete control of my body, and then it hit me: it's never personal. When people in Hollywood love you, it's not about you. It's about what they think they are getting from you. And when they don't love you, it's not about you either. It's about what they think they are *not* getting from you. So, whether they love you or not, it was never about you.

This realization was so deep and thanks to it, I have been able to navigate LA with so much love. Realizing this is an incredible place where reality is augmented so we can all heal big.

I feel incredibly fortunate to have called Los Angeles home for the past 20 years. This city serves as the ultimate training ground for enlightenment. Just envision this: a metropolis brimming with creative souls who have left their origins behind in pursuit of greatness. These individuals are undeniably talented, yet a significant portion of them grapple with a relentless need for validation and recognition.

In my view, residing in LA offers two distinct paths: either succumbing to the ego's insatiable hunger for validation, forever chasing external approval to fill the void of feeling "not good enough," or making a deliberate choice to perceive life as a game, refusing to take it too seriously while mastering its intricacies.

My spiritual mentor, Byron Katie, once shared a profound insight: "Human beings don't love; they want something." Now, this isn't to suggest that people are purely transactional or devoid of care. Rather, it's an invitation to reflect on how we perceive others. If we view them through a lens of transaction and insincerity, we'll inevitably find evidence to support that perspective. However, if we choose to see them as inherently innocent individuals striving to navigate life as best they can, we'll also experience that sense of compassion and understanding.

Byron Katie also once remarked, "I can walk into a room and know that everyone loves me. I just don't expect them to realize it yet." Her words carry a profound truth about the nature of love. In essence, she suggests that deep down, we all harbor love for one another, even if we're not consciously aware of it. When we tap into this understanding and approach interactions with love and compassion, we naturally feel uplifted and aligned. It's through this feeling of goodness and resonance that we recognize the presence of love within ourselves and extend it to others.

Reaching a level of peace at that Hollywood party, where I realized that the behavior of others wasn't a reflection of my worth, marked a significant milestone for me. It was a moment of triumph over my surroundings, demonstrating my ability to maintain inner harmony despite external challenges.

One could say that overcoming our environment is the "manipulation of our narration of life." It's the ultimate power move when using the STFU Method. When we choose to make something mean what we want it to mean, we win. Not only that, but it's also the most powerful habit that we can practice. Together, let's support one another in awakening to this transformative potential.

The more we narrate what we want to make things mean, the more joy and peace we will find. The more joy and peace we find, the better we will feel and the healthier we will be.

And the best part is, our positive outlook on life becomes contagious. By radiating positivity and embracing our life narrative, we naturally uplift those around us. People are drawn to our positive energy, and being in our presence becomes a joyous experience for them.

I'm not suggesting that you become the STFU police. Instead, embody the principles of the STFU Method in your daily life. Be the individual who refrains from contributing to negative discourse. Approach situations with compassion and empathy. Create a nurturing environment where your friends feel valued and supported. And occasionally, when appropriate and rooted in love and generosity, gently encourage them to STFU.

THIRTY-NINE

A "NO" is a "YES" to Something Else

> ❚❚ *A door closed doesn't mean you're trapped; it just means you have to find another way in."*

> - *Dave Asprey*

The notion of the "unknown" is something I've been familiar with for as long as I can remember. It truly resonates with me in every aspect of my life.

Embracing the unknown is a constant journey, one marked by a transition from discomfort to appreciation. I think we all constantly face uncertainty, longing for control over outcomes. As I've emphasized previously, relinquishing control doesn't come naturally to us; it requires deliberate effort and the practice of techniques like the STFU Method.

What if we reframed our perspective on the unknown, seeing it not as something to fear or avoid, but as something to eagerly anticipate. Instead of dreading uncertainty, what if we embraced it as an exciting journey full of possibilities and surprises.

A "NO' is a 'YES' to something else." This phrase underscores the potency of rejection, suggesting that a denial can be just as impactful, if not more so, than an affirmation. A 'NO' not only directs us towards alternative possibilities, but also reveals our degree of attachment to our initial desires. It's not about dissuading pursuit of our goals, but rather acknowledging that what we seek may not always align with what's truly best for us in the present moment. Perhaps there's a superior opportunity awaiting us, and it's only through encountering a 'NO' that we'll uncover it.

Now, more than ever, I appreciate finding myself in less-than-ideal situations to observe my reactions. How do I respond when faced with adversity? Like a canceled flight announced by the airline representative? Or how do I handle unexpected setbacks, such as developing a cold sore on the night of an important date? These moments offer invaluable insights into my character and resilience.

It was a remarkable moment when I realized how differently I reacted in a new environment compared to my past self. For example, I was vacationing for New Year's Eve and met someone incredible during the trip. It was literally like a love story. But then, on the third day, I got a cold sore. Mind you, I hadn't had a cold sore in about six years, and it was just the perfect time (meaning it was awful). Without going into any big drama, I moved swiftly, asking the friends who were hosting me for vacation if they had some medication for it. They happened to have the most powerful stuff around. Talk about being lucky and overcoming my environment. Normally, having a cold sore in this kind of situation would send me off the deep end, but not this time. This is where I got to see the incredible personal growth that I have experienced. There was no shame, no panic, no nothing, really. The STFU Method didn't stop me from asking for help, its not designed for that. In fact, it made me go to the straight to a helpful source, and they gave me what I needed, the magical cream.

What fun it is to see who you have become via the STFU Method in real-time. You become more efficient, strategic, and kind with the things that you want to say. I always tell people I love that I want to be the kind of person who could be swimming in pig shit and at the same time asking, "Who's wearing the Chanel Number Five I smell?" That's overcoming the environment.

Engaging in the STFU Method naturally cultivates within you a profound appreciation for the intricacies of reality. It will allow you to recognize that every twist and turn is ultimately leading you towards your highest good.

FORTY

Embrace Authenticity

❚❚ *True freedom comes when you release the need to control every outcome and trust in the unfolding of life's journey."*

- *Chris Williamson*

As I've emphasized previously, our innate inclination towards control and survival often leads us to manipulate and coerce others into conforming to our expectations. However, with consistent practice of the STFU Method, these tendencies gradually diminish, allowing us to relinquish the need for control and embrace the authenticity of those around us. Rather than imposing our desires onto others, we learn to appreciate and honor their unique essence, fostering deeper and more meaningful connections. This shift in perspective enables us to experience the full richness of human relationships, free from the constraints of manipulation and coercion.

Now, I am not saying that if you are a parent, you shouldn't discipline your child. And you know how I feel about parting ways with friends or relationships that you feel you have completed. But the more that you use the STFU Method, the more you will realize that you love people exactly how they are. You will see how you have no reason to change them because they are exactly who they should be.

Do you think this is nuts? I mean it. Hey, you can love a person from afar and know in your truest of hearts that they are doing the best they can with the tools they have. You will know that loving someone doesn't mean you have to even talk to them. I have so many beautiful friends that I no longer communicate with. I have realized that not speaking with them doesn't discount the beautiful experiences that we had together.

I had a friend years ago who took his life. He was going through a lot of depression from a drug addiction. He left me a suicide note and, in the note, he wrote one of the simplest yet most profound things I have ever read, which I will always remember in his honor. He wrote, "Please remember us by all the good times we had, not how it ended."

I think that's what happens in life. We tend to remember how a friendship ended by their last chapter and not so much by the good times. The only place where that's not true is when we are thinking of getting back with an ex-partner; in that situation, for some reason we seem to forget all the reasons why it ended. And thank god we have our closest friends to remind us.

I used to struggle with letting people go and have them "leave my life" until I started seeing how beautiful it was to complete a chapter. Now, I let my memories marinate, thinking about how amazing those people were in my life. I think about how I honor their paths by respecting that they are taking care of what's in front of them right now, even though it's not me.

That's the thing, right? In this 3D world, we have limited time to create amazing new connections and care for ourselves. If we don't let some people go, we are not creating room for amazing new people to come in.

What a beautiful world, filled with people, as we use the STFU Method to narrate them perfectly. They might not be perfect for us, but they are perfect for who they are in this moment.

The other day, I was talking about a friend who has "a lot" of energy. I found myself praising him for how much energy he has instead of saying any possible negative things about him. The whole world could look at his behavior and declare it unconventional and wrong. But you can be the one who praises someone for being the way they are: especially if they are different from you. How great is that?

Embracing and celebrating the differences in others is a beautiful aspect of personal growth and inner work. As we become aligned with the STFU Method, we cultivate a sense of acceptance and appreciation for the unique qualities and quirks of those around us. What once irritated us, now could be perceived as endearing or simply no longer bothersome. By releasing resistance and judgment, we open ourselves up to deeper connections and genuine relationships based on love and understanding

FORTY-ONE

Destiny Vs. Free Will

❚❚ *Free will is your power to choose,*
and destiny is what happens when
you make those choices."

- Mel Robbins

Since I started to learn more about the quantum field, which is the field where all possibilities exist, I began to understand what the concept of destiny versus free will really means. Everything in life is an example or a metaphor to something else. I love how metaphors exist everywhere in life to explain everything, almost to confirm that we are all a type of simulation.

If our existence on this Earth is a school, it makes sense that if you get your major in fashion versus architecture, you will get different experiences and lessons. What if our lives could be broken into a destiny-type school? But, within that school, we choose what classes to take (free will).

I think in life, there is a script, just like the one a writer makes for a movie. But then, just like when you are shooting a film, you can change the direction of the movie. So, one can look at life and see that destiny plays a part. But what if the way we think about life can open up unlikely paths? What if some incredible roads are only available because we use the STFU Method? I know it takes some discipline, but I think that we can collapse destiny and free will. You can access unlikely available paths because you broke the patterns that were keeping you away from them.

Certainly, a plethora of versions of you could live in the quantum field of your different possibilities. And I can tell you that the more energy you put into the things that you want, the easier you will reach your goals. At the same time, how you are wired will affect how much access you have to these experiences.

Indeed, the STFU Method serves as a powerful tool for rewiring our perception of the world and transforming our internal landscape. Through this method, we interrupt the habitual patterns of negative self-talk and limiting beliefs, allowing us to create new neural pathways that align with positivity and empowerment. As we shift our focus towards gratitude, affirmation, and visualization, we activate the brain's ability to produce feel-good chemicals, fostering a more optimistic outlook on life. With consistent practice, the STFU Method empowers us to cultivate a reality filled with joy, abundance, and fulfillment.

By deciding to see the world the way you want to see it, instead of letting life dictate how the world is occurring to you, you will become one with your intention. You will experience the life that you want to experience. Every NO will feel like a YES, and every moment will be a dance with the unknown that will bring you into a position of power. What fun it will be to love your life exactly how it is and create the possibility of transformation at the same time.

Imagine experiencing a life where you don't feel the need to change it. I am not crazy, I swear. That is the way that life feels for me, a lot of times. Sometimes I miss a connecting flight or don't get the opportunity I wanted. But now, there is an awakened inner system. Even though I don't get that thing I want, my inner knowing sees that this moment is the right one for me, exactly the way it is. This moment is the one I want because this is the one that is happening.

By the way, I am not saying you can't change things. In fact, you will be able to change things even faster if you are not resisting them. The other day, I traveled through a foreign airport and wanted to go to the priority lounge. Long story short, I did not have my Priority card (an airport lounge service), and they needed the expiration date on my membership, which I didn't have. At first, I noticed I was very calm explaining my point of view, but the ticket agent was not helping me. I could feel the part of me that wanted to make her wrong. She suggested I go online to find the information she needed. As I started doing that, the web page got stuck. My frustration was on the rise, but I had awareness and mindfulness, while this was happening to me. Sure, I was running my reactive program, but I could be separated from the program. I was definitely not unconscious, although I did feel heated. I stopped and knew that I needed to let this go. I know better now than to allow this experience to grab ahold of me.

I proceeded to exit the situation and went into the regular area in the airport, where I consciously noticed it was not bad at all. I even noticed a phone charging station, which was my biggest consideration at that point. I fully felt like I let it go. Then, magically, once I felt peace for letting it go, I thought to myself, why don't I just call the number for Priority and try to speak with someone? I called and got someone from their team on the phone to let me know the expiration date I needed, and I was able to get into the priority area.

I can say that knowing I needed to let go of the situation gave me the freedom of creativity to decide to call and solve the problem. I feel so blessed now that the STFU Method has made such a huge impact in my life. I constantly feel a state of grace with everything that life throws my way. This doesn't mean I don't have reactive moments, but the refractory periods (periods of upset) are much shorter and mindful. The unknown always takes care of us and gives us an amazing opportunity to show up as our best selves. The STFU Method will be your greatest partner in crime in rewiring you into becoming the ultimate machine that will always see the glass half super full.

FORTY-TWO

Perspective and Perception

❚❚ *Perspective is not just about what*
we see, but how we choose to see it.
It's the lens through which we view the
world, shaping our reality and guiding
our actions."

- Danny Morel

I love these two P's. First of all, both of these words are essential to remember. What I love the most is their subtle difference and how one helps to define the other. We will never be able to be out of the perception game because we see everything through the lens of our minds. At the same time, knowing that we are seeing everything through our own perception gives us the freedom to know that what we see is not the truth. We know that everything we see is through our specific lens of life. That is the key.

When I talk about perspective, on the other hand, I am talking about how we could have access to see everything from a panoramic view. What do I mean by that? Let's say you have a friend who can't help falling in love with the wrong guy. You think the guys she dates will never take your friend seriously. You also feel your friend dates these guys for the "wrong reasons." Maybe you feel that she shouldn't date based on how wealthy these guys are. Or maybe you don't agree with how obsessively she pursues men in general. Whatever the issue is for you, in this case, you can only see everything through your perception (through your lens).

Let's say you were to ask someone else for their opinion about your friend's dating behavior. Maybe they would not think that she is aggressively pursuing men. Maybe they think she is smart for thinking about financial security for her future when it comes to picking men to date. That is how they look at your friend's dating behavior, through their lens, their perception.

When I think about perspective, I think more of empathy for other human beings. While applying perspective, I distinctly think I can suspend my perception for a moment and get into the other person's world.

I was just at the airport (I know so many of my enlightened spiritual moments happen to me at the airport, I know!). A woman was sitting a few seats away from me, having a normal, intimate conversation on the phone (I could clearly hear everything). I was doing some writing, and it was hard to concentrate while hearing her stories. I decided to move and sit on the floor nearby, where some adorable toddlers starting to fight. I then noticed a girl took the seat right next to the woman, which, in a way, forced the woman to lower her voice quite a bit. Score! I went back to my seat and continued to write.

I also wanted to change my seat on the plane, so I got up and got in line to talk to talk to the ticket agent. As I was waiting, the woman who had been on the phone cut in front of me and said, "I just have a question for her." I quickly replied, "Me too, madam." She realized she was cutting the line in front of me and told me she only needed to know if she was at the right gate. Then she noticed she was in the right place and sat back down. I could tell she recognized that she had gotten in front of me. I was slightly annoyed, remembering how I had to maneuver away from her loud phone conversation. I got a healthy dose of my internal STFU Method.

Ok, so here is the perspective in this situation: the woman who was talking on the phone didn't mean to be loud. She was probably really engaged in speaking with her friend. I remember doing the same thing, talking loudly on the phone in a compromised space. I am sure people around me were quite annoyed with me. Also, when she went to ask the ticket agent a question, I am sure she didn't mean to cut me off. She probably just figured that a super-fast question wouldn't really matter.

By infusing the perspective/perception formula into my life, I can see perfection in everyone's actions, including mine. That woman did what she did, and I created all the different interpretations of her actions.

There is nothing I can accuse someone of doing that I haven't done in the past myself or at some point in some capacity. That is true awareness. Maybe it wasn't to such a high degree, but I have done it somehow. The STFU

Method will empower you to cut the cords on these patterns, so you move swiftly into intentional experiences. It is time to stop being a victim of what people do and stop allowing your negative interpretations dictate how you feel. The STFU Method will be the ultimate guide for you, and before you know it, the life of your dreams won't be able to be turned off.

FORTY-THREE

Words Hold Power

❚❚ *Where attention goes, energy flows, and results show."*

- Vishen Lakhiani

I love how spelling comes from the word "spells." Words have such power, and as we have all experienced, sometimes we can't take them back. It's like if I tell someone they're ugly and then I say: "Oh, I was just kidding." It doesn't really work that way.

At the same time, the power of words is undeniable. In the STFU Method, words are the ultimate key to life creation. By transforming what you say and what you *don't* say, you will be able to transform your life from the inside out. By adopting the STFU Method, we reverse engineer: "Believe, thought, word," and we go backwards. We stop the words, which will minimize the thoughts, thus eradicating the beliefs. What we say about people and how we narrate the world, is a big conglomerate of habits we need to rewire. But don't worry; it starts with one small step: the STFU Method.

Life is amazing and it will constantly put you in situations where you will see your power. Life is the playground that calls forth your greatness to show up and take center stage. Now, your greatness will not always look so "great." But, there are always opportunities for your greatness to show up. I am sure you have found yourself in the same situations many times, thinking, "Why is this happening to me again?" It's almost as if life is playing a beautiful game to show us who we are in the moment. Life gives us all the opportunities we require to play out the same scenario, over and over again, and make a different choice.

Now, life doesn't really care if we make a different choice or not. It's just the stage holding the space for us to perform. We are the actors in the play; we get to dictate how we perform that night.

When you talk about something and give it your attention, you also give it the energy to grow. However, deciding not to talk about the things that bother you doesn't mean you're ignoring them. In fact, you may handle them better by directly addressing them with the person involved in the situation rather than verbalizing them to everyone. I am not a trained therapist or counselor, but I am a very communicative human being. I know first-hand the disservice that I have done to myself by telling the same traumatizing story over and over again to a multitude of people.

I am introducing to you a way out. One that will hold you with love and grace while keeping you accountable as you transform your life.

The STFU Method will be your greatest ally in breaking your patterns and truly give you what you want. It will break your addiction to your emotional states. Breaking this addiction will create a crack in your life's wall of beliefs. And as you know, once there is a crack in the wall, it will keep getting bigger. Trust yourself, trust the process. The STFU Method is the crack in the wall that you have been waiting for. This crack will grow, giving you full access to the life of your dreams.

FORTY-FOUR

Looking for Validation

> ❚❚ *True belonging only happens when we present our authentic, imperfect selves to the world, our sense of belonging can never be greater than our level of self-acceptance."*
>
> *- Brené Brown*

We are born with an innate desire to want love, approval, and appreciation. I think this is something that all human beings come hardwired with since day one. Validation is something that comes up subconsciously in most conversations and is ramped up in our culture. We tell stories, and we constantly look for agreement. If we don't find agreement, we tend to feel a level of depletion and incompletion.

While you are getting your sea legs going with the STFU Method, if you are caught up in a conversation where someone is gossiping or looking for validation, sit there and STFU. Don't add to the conversation. Feel free to change the subject if you can, and if you are forced to say something, say, "I hear you." It's fine for other people to think you agree with them, but deep inside, you will know that you are not.

With the STFU Method, the need for validation diminishes over time, leading to fewer situations where it's sought after. Conversations take on a more elevated tone, free from gossip or negativity in your presence. Your charisma and charm will remain intact, but will be infused with a playful and youthful energy. You will remind others of their innate goodness, capacity for love and compassion. Through your example, you will inspire people to feel more love and connection with each other, all thanks to the transformative power of the STFU Method

FORTY-FIVE

Be Your Own Publicist

❚❚ *Your biggest limitations are the ones you place on yourself. Break free from self-imposed boundaries and watch your potential soar."*

- *Codie Sanchez*

I've lived in LA for the last 20 years working in the entertainment industry. I have come to know a lot of publicists. A publicist, by definition, is someone tasked with safeguarding an individual's personal brand. It's common practice for celebrities to enlist the expertise of publicists to garner media attention and shape the narrative they wish to convey to their audience.

The issue arises when we unwittingly become our own worst publicists, inadvertently undermining our own character in the eyes of others.

Just the other day, while chatting with my friend Maria, the topic of our mutual friend Kevin came up. I mentioned to her that Kevin had recently moved in with his girlfriend, and they seemed to be thriving together. Maria's surprise was palpable; she couldn't believe that Kevin not only had a girlfriend but had taken such a significant step in their relationship. To quote Maria, she exclaimed, "Kevin has a girlfriend? Unlucky in love Kevin?"

In that moment, a vivid recollection surfaced of Kevin frequently expressing his struggles with finding love in Los Angeles. He'd often regale us with tales of disappointment, lamenting the challenges of meeting a compatible partner, and citing instances of being stood up by women. It dawned on me that Kevin's own narrative about his romantic misfortunes had sculpted the perception others held of him.

What's intriguing about this scenario is that Kevin's reputation regarding his love life was entirely crafted by his own words. He was the architect of his own public persona, continually venting to us about his "girl problems," inadvertently solidifying the image others had of him.

Now, let me be clear: I'm not suggesting we put on airs or pretend to be something we're not. However, we also don't need to broadcast our romantic woes to the world like we're issuing a press release.

To put it plainly, we become known for the things we constantly complain about. So instead of crafting a public persona centered on what we'd rather avoid, why don't we collectively opt for a little more discretion like shutting the fuck up?

Consider this scenario: You find yourself stuck in a frustrating pattern, such as getting canceled on the night of a date. Let's say it's the third time in a row. The last thing you should do is pick up the phone and start lamenting to your friends about it. By doing so, you're only reinforcing that pattern. Remember our crash course in quantum physics: you, as the observer, have the power to shape reality. By vocalizing and magnifying a negative pattern, you're unwittingly making it more entrenched.

Instead of airing your grievances, try reframing the situation. Consider the notion that rejection may, in fact, be protection. If someone cancels on you last minute, perhaps they weren't the right match for you to begin with. It's a blessing in disguise, sparing you from investing time and resources into a possibly very expensive dinner.

I understand that there are moments when we feel compelled to share our problems with others, almost as if it's an emotional addiction. However, as I've mentioned before, if you truly need to confide in someone, choose just one trusted person and pour your heart out. Also, keep in mind that breaking free from the habit of constant complaining may seem challenging at first, but it becomes easier over time.

Consider embracing your inherent greatness. The next time someone pays you a compliment and you feel a pang of discomfort, resist the urge to downplay it. Instead, take a moment to graciously accept it with a simple "thank you." You may be surprised by how uplifting this can be for both you and the person giving the compliment.

Furthermore, cease to tarnish your own character by allowing yourself to be defined by traits or experiences you'd rather not highlight. Become your own champion by taking charge of how you present yourself to the world. Be the architect of your own narrative by being your own greatest publicist.

FORTY-SIX

Practice What You Preach

❚❚ *I don't know shit about you, so guess what I do...I shut the fuck up"*

- David Goggins

After practicing the STFU Method for so long, it's hard for me not to drink my own Kool-Aid or believe that it's my way or the highway. What I mean by that is that the STFU Method doesn't make sense unless you are being compassionate and kind to yourself and others. There were many times when I would jump the gun to tell someone to STFU when they complained about their lives. But how could I say that "everything is exactly how it should be" if I told someone else to STFU? Well, I learned this the hard and the right way.

The other day, I was with one of my best friends, and we were catching up. He had recently posted on social media about having a problem with an authority figure. I told him I saw the post and wanted to hear what happened. He hesitated a bit but eventually told me. As he told the story, I could feel myself anxiously waiting for my turn to talk. When he finished, I didn't even wait two seconds before I jumped in and said something like, "Well, you know, this is your pattern, and you need to use the STFU Method!"

Let's just say that my "enlightened words" were not received as such. My friend paused very calmly, looked me in the eyes, and said, "This is exactly why I don't come to you anymore." He said he couldn't tell me things that happened in his life without feeling judged by me. He was dealing with a traumatizing situation and wasn't seeking my feedback or advice. He said he wanted a safe place to land and tell his story, and I hadn't been a safe place for him, in a long time...ouch.

I can't begin to tell you what a profound impact this had on me. I am so grateful to him.

Somewhere along the way with this STFU journey, I had forgotten that the greatest thing I could be for anyone is a safe space. That doesn't mean I need to be anyone's therapist, but more importantly, I don't need to be the STFU police either. I read once that being a good teacher is knowing where the student is. I certainly don't always feel like I need to be a teacher, but I do feel I could always be a safe space.

I'm not dwelling on what transpired. It was a moment, driven by good intentions. I expressed gratitude for his insightful words and acknowledged that our conversation would serve as the final chapter of this book. Every life experience, including this one, has contributed to the creation of this book. My aim is to share a toolkit and anecdotes that have profoundly impacted my life. I hope that these lessons and stories will resonate with you and assist you on your own journey.

My quest for wholeness will be eternal. As I go through life, I notice certain things detonate during different seasons of my life. I don't do the work to "fix" myself or to have it all figured out when "bad" things happen. I do the work because I love it and because I love people. I can honestly say that I don't think I am broken or need any fixing. I also don't think anyone else is broken or needs fixing. To see the world as whole is to see me as whole, and to see me as whole is to see the world as whole.

Both my parents died of cancer, and it ignited a desire in me to take care of my health and my emotional state, both for me and for my sister. And after a while, I realized that my desire got even bigger. Now I am out to take care of my fellow man, to take care of the flock.

My parents followed the powerful flight plan of their destiny. They died exactly where and when they were supposed to. But they also did not die in vain. They died to show us the gift of life. They died to offer us the possibility of a more peaceful life. To me, there is nothing wrong with death; in fact, it's the most natural phase of life we will all encounter. But, while I am alive, I will choose life. I will choose life by constantly, consciously, and intentionally choosing love. Love may not always manifest as a smile and gratitude; at times, it demands we navigate through tears and anguish—both physical and emotional. We must always remember that we are all doing the best we can at every precise moment. Sometimes our best is not going to look that great. But it is still a manifestation of the divine and it is perfect.

Remember that our greatest pain is also our greatest teacher. Life is always going to help us grow the muscles that we need to build, in order to get, what we came here to get.

FORTY-SEVEN

Imperfectly Perfect

> **66** *Discover the magic in the mundane & find stillness in simplicity. Your joy isn't out there...it's right here."*
>
> *- Andre Duqum*

I vividly recall my teenage years, a time when I wrestled with the age-old question: "Am I on the right path?" It's a query that seems to possess a mystical ability to haunt us throughout all of our lives, and unequivocally, I believe the answer is always yes.

Now, this isn't to say that we don't harbor desires and aspirations to become the best version of ourselves and break free from patterns that no longer serve us. It's crucial to acknowledge that wholeheartedly accepting our current circumstances is what provides the fertile ground for us to journey towards our desired destinations.

While I thought I had penned the final chapter of my book, this remarkable journey has been guided by some extraordinary individuals, such as my dear friend Selina, whose profound insights have enriched the tapestry of my narrative.

Upon finishing the manuscript, Selina graciously offered her feedback, expressing a sentiment that resonated deeply with me. She felt there was something missing, something vital to tie the entire book together. She compared the ending I had chosen to a "Scooby-Doo" finale—a rushed attempt to wrap up loose ends, leaving a lingering sense of incompleteness.

Selina possesses a fervent dedication to adhering to the rules of any method. However, she found herself grappling with one of the commandments in the STFU method—that of confiding in only one person about your problems.

The truth of the matter is that the STFU method is merely a suggestion, a guideline that has proven effective for me but may not necessarily fit everyone's circumstances. It's essential to allow yourself some flexibility throughout the process and not become too rigid with the verbiage of the method. If you find yourself inspired to follow any of the guidelines, remember that they don't have to be executed to the letter.

For instance, if you're mindful about limiting the number of people you confide your troubles to, even if it's just a handful, that's a significant achievement. And if you end up confiding in a few more, that's okay too. Perhaps without the guidance of the book, you would have shared your troubles with a multitude of people, inadvertently casting yourself as the ultimate victim of your own life. But now, you've made a conscious decision to change that narrative.

I can't stress enough how strongly I believe that each one of us is navigating this game of life to the best of our abilities. It's crucial to extend compassion to ourselves first and foremost. We're all trying our best in each moment.

Humanity has a remarkable way of showing up unconditionally. Meaning that what you see is what you get. Sometimes we're more fragile, and other times we're tougher. But what truly matters is that we're all here. We're coexisting in this perfect moment in time. We may not all be friends or even make efforts to align our vibes, but I do believe we owe it to the planet to embrace our differences and "agree to disagree."

As we prepare to conclude our journey together, I leave you with this: we are all... imperfectly perfect. The only measure of perfection that truly matters is the reflection staring back at you in the mirror, both inside and out, exactly the way it is. The sooner you embrace your imperfect perfection, the sooner you'll recognize it in others.

Now, let's not get it twisted. As much as I'll remind you of your imperfect perfection, and love you for it, I'll also gently nudge you, with unicorns and sugar on top, to always and forever... SHUT THE FUCK UP.